D0903829

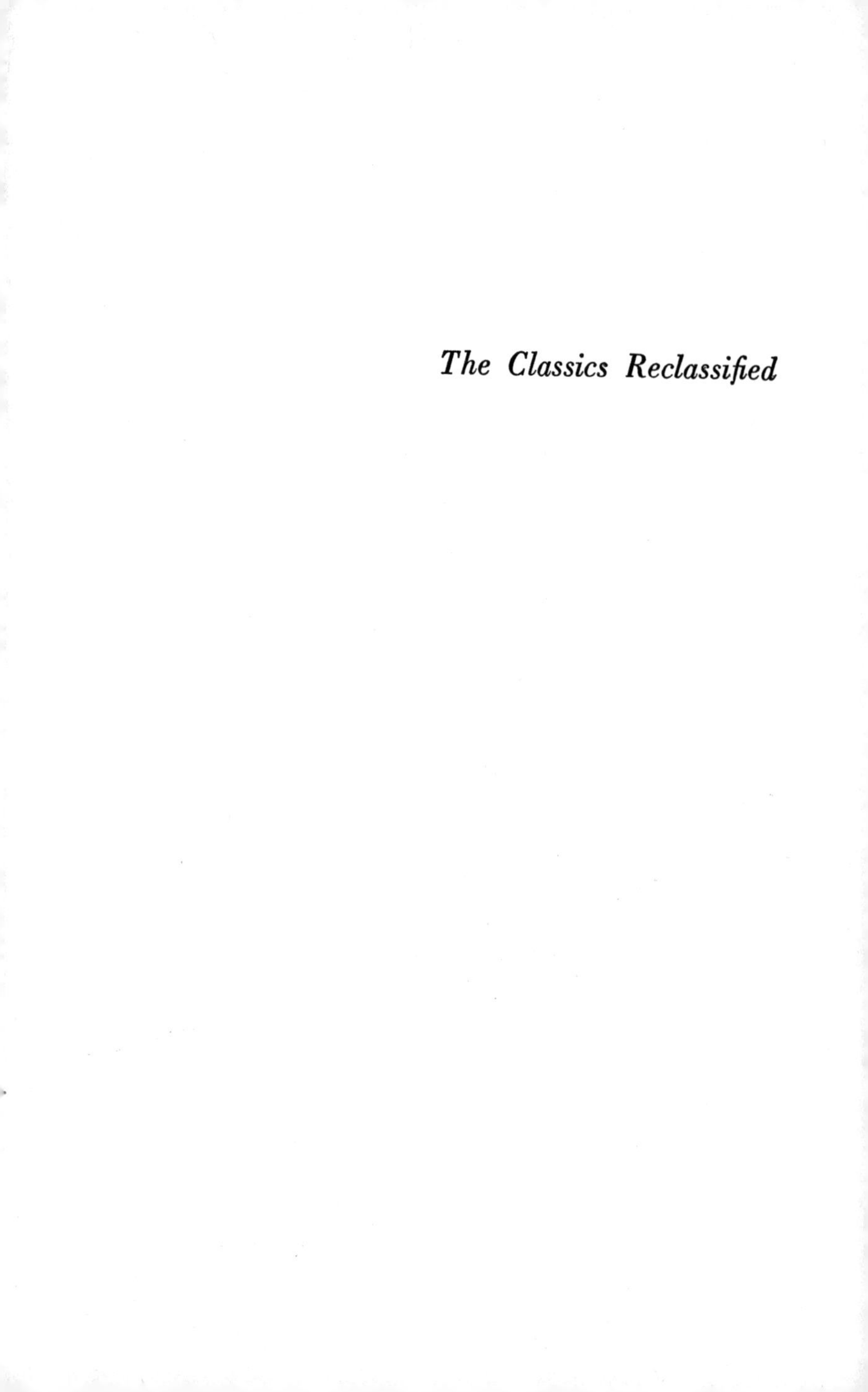

The Classics Reclassified

THE

CLASSICS RECLASSIFIED

IN WHICH CERTAIN FAMOUS BOOKS ARE NOT SO MUCH DIGESTED AS INDIGESTED, TOGETHER WITH MERCIFULLY BRIEF BIOGRAPHIES OF THEIR AUTHORS, A FEW UNNECESSARY FOOTNOTES, AND QUESTIONS WHICH IT MIGHT BE HELPFUL NOT TO ANSWER

by Richard Armour

Nostalgically Illustrated by CAMPBELL GRANT

McGRAW-HILL BOOK COMPANY, INC.
New York Toronto London

THE CLASSICS RECLASSIFIED

Library of Congress Catalog Card Number: 60-14610

First Printing, September, 1960
Second Printing, January, 1961
Third Printing, March, 1962
Fourth Printing, May, 1963
Fifth Printing, March, 1966
Sixth Printing, February, 1967
Seventh Printing, December, 1967
Eighth Printing, June, 1969
Ninth Printing, October, 1970

02256

Dedicated

to that amazing device, the Required Reading List, better even than artificial respiration for keeping dead authors alive.

Contents

HOMER

Almost nothing is known about Homer, which explains why so much has been written about him. We do not know, for instance, whether Homer was his first name or his last name. After all, Horace was Horace's middle name, so you never can tell.

Nevertheless, it seems well established that Homer was born in Greece—a lucky break for Greek literature. He is said to have been born in seven cities, which indicates how his mother kept on the move. He is also said to have been born in six centuries, apparently after a number of false starts.

Herodotus and others have described Homer as blind,

although internal evidence in his poems suggests that he had an eye for the ladies. He is thought to have been a poverty-stricken poet, unable to make a living at his craft, and thus seems remarkably modern.[1] Whether he ever married is not known, though one critic seems positive that he remained a bachelor. "The author of the *Iliad* and the *Odyssey*," this scholar opines, "was a single person."

We can only conjecture about Homer's life in Athens. Reference to the "Homeric cycle" suggests that he got about on some sort of wheel, perhaps of his own invention.[2] He must have been a familiar figure, pedaling around the Parthenon and coasting recklessly down the steep roads of the Acropolis. Athenians kept a wary eye out for him, often shouting to one another: "Look out! Here comes the blind poet riding no hands!"

[1] It seems silly for scholars to argue about when Homer flourished. Obviously he never did.

[2] See Pope's famous remark: "Homer is universally allowed to have had the greatest invention of any writer whatsoever."

The Homeric cycle

Far from being one of the pillars of Athens, a city that had plenty of them, Homer seems to have been a slovenly type. We are told that Pisistratus, tyrant of Athens between 560 and 527 B.C., was "the first to arrange in their present order the books of Homer, which were previously in confusion." It took a tyrant to straighten out the mess he left, his mother and the local librarian having given up in despair.

The house in which Homer lived has never been identified. What might have been a source of income has thus become a source of regret to Greek travel bureaus and Athenian guides. Indeed the only clue to the environment in which he wrote is the fact that he sometimes used the Attic dialect. For centuries, researchers have poked around under the eaves of ancient buildings, looking for manuscripts.

Most scholars believe that Homer wrote nothing down, perhaps not wishing to leave any incriminating evidence. Instead, he recited his poems on street corners, in the market place, and on those increasingly rare occasions when he was invited to someone's house for dinner. It took him about twenty hours to recite the whole of the *Iliad*, not counting interruptions for applause and threats of violence. By starting at dawn, he could get through shortly after midnight, which left him about four hours' sleep before commencing the *Odyssey*. When he became famous, the marquee on the Parthenon announced "Homer in the *Iliad* and the *Odyssey*," the first double feature in the history of the theater.

This was the beginning of the Oral Tradition, which finally died out, in 329 B.C., during an epidemic of laryngitis.

Homer's works are epics, which means that they begin

in the middle of things and keep the reader confused to the very end. The characters are of heroic mold, probably from standing out in the rain all these years. There are many epic digressions, for Homer's mind wandered considerably in his later years.[1] Finally, there is epic sweep, a device used to whisk characters off the earth when the author is through with them.

The marked difference between the styles of his two great epics has given rise to the theory that Homer was a man when he wrote the *Iliad* and a woman when he wrote the *Odyssey*. This is the sort of thing that makes life difficult for a biographer, but not nearly so perplexing as it must have been for his friends.

If Homer was born in the ninth century B.C., he probably died in that century or in the eighth, since people lived backward in those days. Gilbert Murray speaks cheerfully of "the condition of Homer in the second century B.C.," but one doubts that it was any too good.

[1] Along with Homer, as he went from town to town.

The Iliad

The *Iliad* is not a poem about the ill. It is about Ilium, which is another name for Troy and not the new chemical added to a toothpaste. More specifically, it is about the wrath of Achilles, a Greek warrior who as an infant was held by the heel and dipped in the Styx by his mother. By dunking him in this manner, she thought to make him invulnerable (if she didn't drown him), but clumsily left an unwashed place on his heel, where she was holding onto the little squirmer.

Achilles is not angry at his mother, however, but at Agamemnon, one of the Greek leaders in the Trojan War. Since the war has been going on for more that nine years

A ten-year war

(it is a ten-year war, of which only a few weeks remain), nerves are understandably frayed.

Each book of the *Iliad* is prefaced by a summary which tempts one not to read any further. The summary at the beginning of Book I tells "How Agamemnon and Achilles fell out at the siege of Troy," but since it does not tell what they fell out of, one is forced to read on. It seems that Achilles fleet of foot had won Briseis of the fair cheeks along with some other spoils of war, and now Agamemnon of the hairy chest wants her for his own tent.

Since wide-ruling Agamemnon outranks him, narrow-ruling Achilles has no choice but to "draw his keen blade from his thigh." [1] But just as he is about to fight for his property, the bright-eyed goddess Athene is sent by the white-armed goddess Hera to stay the strong-armed mortal Achilles.

"Hold thou thine hand," Athene orders him, which of course makes fighting difficult, if not impossible. It was a close call for Agamemnon, who had wangled a direct commission because of a connection with the royal family and is no match for a professional soldier like Achilles.

"Thou swoln with wine, thou with face of a dog," Achilles says descriptively of Agamemnon. Athene may hold back his sword, but she is powerless to check his flow of epithets. Achilles threatens to pull his Myrmidons out of the battle and go home to Phthia, which Agamemnon can't even pronounce.

Up rises tongue-happy Nestor, a wise old Greek who knows almost everything except when to stop talking. He deems it unfortunate, of a truth, that the two warriors should be wroth. So persuasively does he speak that by the time he has finished, Achilles and Agamemnon hate each

[1] A lesser man would have used a scabbard.

other as much as ever, but the reader is several pages nearer the end.

That very day Agamemnon sends a couple of his trigger men, Talthybios of the scarred face and Eurybates of the greasy thumb, to fetch Briseis of the fair cheeks, and Achilles, son of Peleus, gives her up with no more than a deep sigh and a last lingering look. When she is gone, however, he betakes himself to the seashore and makes moan as only a Greek warrior can.

"Mother," he cries out, "he hath taken away my meed of honor," which is a classical euphemism for a well-built damsel.

His mother has no difficulty hearing him, although she is down in the depths of the sea. She is the silver-footed Thetis, a sea deity, who feels better in a damp climate. After Achilles tells her in detail about his troubles with Agamemnon (which gives the reader who did not get it the first time a second chance), Thetis silver-foots it up to Olympus to speak to the head man, Zeus the cloud-gatherer, who has just come in from a hard day of harvesting the cirri and cumuli. Clasping Zeus by the knees, she wheedles out of him a promise to help Achilles. Zeus is a soft touch, especially around the knees, and he gives Thetis what she wants, though he knows his wife, the ox-eyed Hera, will be displeased.[1] Thetis then leaps from the top of Mount Olympus into the sea, breaking all records for the high dive.

What aegis-bearing[2] Zeus does to help fleet-footed

[1] Zeus was an old roué and sometimes, because of his fondness for assuming the form of animals, an old goat. Greek damsels never knew which livestock would turn out to be Mr. Big.

[2] To save your looking it up, an aegis is a shield. Zeus's aegis was not very functional. It had gold tassels on it, and seems less classical than mid-Victorian.

Zeus—after a hard day of cloud-gathering

Achilles is to incite wide-ruling Agamemnon to attack deep-soiled Troy and see how hard it is to go it alone. To make sure it is a good fight, Zeus sends wind-footed Iris to warn the flowing-haired Trojan leaders about the coming attack. Iris, of course, does not look like Iris but like Priam's son, Polites, a well-mannered chap. In those days a god could take on the shape of anyone, male or female, and some of the female shapes were pretty sensational.

After the recitation of a long list of names and addresses of all the featured warriors, the battle is now ready to be joined. But Paris of the most fair semblance, who had carried off Helen of the white arms and started the whole Trojan fracas in the first place, volunteers to fight Helen's husband, Menelaus of the loud war-cry, in single combat. The winner is to have Helen, white arms and all, and the war will be over. Had they thought of this nine years

Paris at work

he hastes to fetch Paris from his fragrant chamber, where he is being nursed by Helen and is understandably loath to return to the battlefield. He would rather pluck a lyre than twang a bow, any old day.

When Hector enters, Helen begs him to make himself at home, but he says, rather stiffly, "Bid me not sit, Helen." She ought to know that a man in armor finds this awkward. Anyhow, he persuades Paris to put in an appearance. This is the least the man should do who started the war and is going to be celebrated in song and story as the Abductor of Helen.

Then bronze-harnessed Hector drops in on his dear-won wife, even white-armed Andromache, "daughter of great-hearted Eëtion that dwelt beneath wooded Plakos, and was king of the men of Kilikia." (Homer wants us to be sure not to confuse her with all the other Andromaches we know.) With her is Hector's son, Skamandrios, who is nicknamed Astyanax, and probably for some good reason.

A touching domestic scene ensues when Hector reaches out to embrace the lad, who runs wailing to his fair-girdled nurse, frightened by the horsehair crest that nods fiercely from his father's helmet. Trojan warriors should remember to take off their helmets when they come into the house. What do they think the helmet rack by the door is for?

But Hector, though a family man, can tarry only long enough to get a few whiffs of his wife's fragrant bosom, and then he must be off to battle. At least he can come home nights, which is one advantage the Trojans have had over the Greeks for the past nine years.

Now Zeus, who has other things on his mind,[1] remembers the promise he made five or six books back to avenge the wrong done to Achilles by Agamemnon. Rosy-fingered Dawn is barely up and about when Zeus calls a board meeting of the gods. After rapping for attention with a

[1] Mostly women. For a god, he has some very human qualities.

The gods meet

couple of thunderbolts, he orders them to stop helping either the Trojans or the Greeks. Otherwise the war will not come out as Fate has decreed. The gods shrug their shoulders and look innocent.

With Zeus calling the signals, Hector now has one of his best days, hacking and hewing his way almost to the Greeks' ships, which he would surely have burned had he not stopped to make harangue. By the time the harangue is made, it is too dark to fight any more that day. It is also the end of Book VIII.

All this time Achilles has been sulking in his tent. It is a sulk of epic proportions, setting a record never since equaled. Achilles is still sore annoyed at Agamemnon for taking fair-cheeked Briseis away from him. It is wartime, with rationing and all that, and fair-cheeked maidens are hard to come by.

Agamemnon, though he hates to admit it, needs Achilles' help against the Trojans so much that he sends Heaven-

Achilles sulks

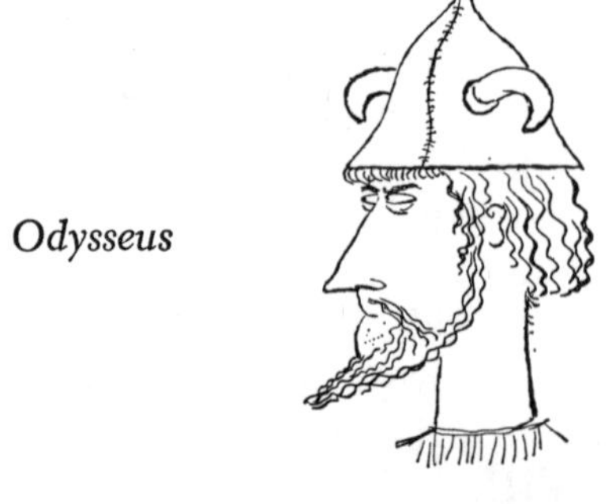

Odysseus

sprung Odysseus (who sprung him, we are not told) to Achilles to tell him he will give him back Briseis, along with twelve horses, seven cities, and his stamp collection, if he will please return to battle, and quick. Odysseus finds Achilles down on the dock strumming a lyre and singing Greek folk songs to an audience of unhappy Myrmidons. Agamemnon's offer leaves Achilles unmoved, and the emissary, even Odysseus of many wiles, returns disconsolately to Agamemnon. He is closely followed by rosy-fingered Dawn.

The next night Nestor, a wise man who is always suggesting that someone else risk his neck, advises Agamemnon to send a couple of scouts into Troy to see what the enemy is up to. It is past midnight, but Agamemnon unhesitatingly routs out Diomedes, even son of Tydeus (there is not an odd son in the *Iliad*), and Odysseus. Since these two worthies are sleeping on a piece of oxhide, with a shield for a pillow, they are easy to awaken.[1]

Diomedes and Odysseus creep into the Trojan camp on

[1] As for Agamemnon's sleeplessness, it was like that of Menelaus, another insomniac, of whom Homer says, "Neither could Sleep settle down on his eyelids." The winking and blinking kept throwing him off.

muffled sandals, capture a counterspy, kill thirteen warriors, unloose horses, and generally act like a couple of characters in a Greek western. Odysseus wears "a helm made of leather, with the white teeth of a boar of flashing tusks arrayed on either side," and the mere sight of him frightens a Trojan corporal into hysterics.

Then follow several books in which, suffice it to say, swords clang, spears fly, and dark blood covers the complaining earth.[1] Great is the carnage, with incidents too gruesome to relate, unless you are an epic poet. (The influence of Homer on Mickey Spillane has, unaccountably, been overlooked.)

At one point the great Hector is wounded by Aias, a lowly Greek who has hardly a consonant to his name, but Zeus patches Hector up and soon has him chasing the foe all the way back to their ships, which he plans to set afire as soon as he can bum a lightning bolt from Zeus.

It is time for Achilles to stop sulking and show some interest in survival.

Patroclus, an emotional youth, throws himself before Achilles, "shedding warm tears, even as a fountain of dark water that down a steep cliff pours its cloudy stream," and begs him to get into the battle. Though he refuses, Achilles is impressed by such lachrymosity, and, wishing to get the fellow out of his tent before it is washed away, offers to lend him his armor. (Fortunately, they are both 42 longs.)

In this borrowed outfit, complete with "studs of silver" which give it a somewhat formal After Six look, Patroclus fares forth, surrounded by a bodyguard of mean-looking Myrmidons. He hacks his way through the Trojans in great style until he runs into Phoebus Apollo, who is a god and should have been disqualified. After Apollo knocks off

[1] In all that din, the earth has trouble making itself heard.

Patroclus' helmet, shatters his spear, and generally softens him up, it is no great task for Hector to run a spear through him and then, in a magnificent speech, talk him to death.

During the whole of Book XVII the Greeks and Trojans fight for the body of Patroclus, which has become not only a symbol but a battlefield. For a while Menelaus stands over the body, as Homer says in one of his more unfortunate similes, "as above a first-born calf standeth lowing its mother, ere then unused to motherhood." By this time Homer was scraping the barrel for poetic figures.

Menelaus

Amidst the melee, Hector, who has always admired Achilles' armor, strips it from the body of Patroclus. This is no easy task, with spears flying overhead and with some of the buttons rusted, but Hector gets it off at last, and leaves poor Pat in his shorts. He can hardly wait to get back to the palace and look at himself in a mirror.

When Achilles hears of the death of Patroclus (and the loss of his suit of armor, which was uninsured), he pulls his hair out by the roots and pours handfuls of dust and ashes on his head and all over his clean shirt, which is a way the Greeks have of showing emotion. He is soon the very picture of unhappiness. But, though his scalp hurts and his teeth grind grittily, he finds that Agamemnon no longer annoys him. With his single-wrath mind, all he can think of is getting his hands on Hector.

Alas, though he would rejoin the fray, Achilles hasn't a thing to wear. He makes moan, and his handmaidens beat their breasts, first one and then the other. Afar on the sea bottom, silver-footed Thetis hears the moaning and thumping and rises to the situation, through many a fathom. Mama always picks out Achilles' clothes for him anyhow, and forthwith hastes to the abode of the Immortals, where the crook-footed god Hephaestus, the village smithy, is banging on his anvil. Hephaestus is called Vulcan for short, fortunately.[1]

Thetis orders her son a shield, helmet, cuirass, greaves, and ankle pieces—a complete suit of armor with two pairs of bronze pants. Though it is a rush order, Hephaestus takes his time. The shield, for instance, he embellishes until it is a museum piece, with pictures on it of the earth, the heavens, the sea, the signs of the zodiac, scenes of battles and sports, farmers plowing, feasts, sacrifices, people playing musical instruments, lions eating cattle, youths and maidens dancing, and so on. Hephaestus could easily have carved the Lord's Prayer on the head of a pin, if he had known the Lord's Prayer.

As soon as it is delivered, Achilles dons his new suit and strides aleap[2] of his horse, Xanthos of the glancing feet. Everyone else having made a speech, Xanthos now also makes a brief statement, full of horse sense and showing a creditable knowledge of mythology. Achilles then heads

[1] Imagine our having to hephaestusize something, instead of vulcanizing it.

[2] No clichés in *this* book.

Makes a brief statement

into the thick of battle, thinning it out considerably. He kills one Trojan after another, but seldom before a long discourse on his victim's ancestors, since he is something of a show-off when it comes to genealogy. The River Xanthos, which has the same name as Achilles' horse and also can talk, is getting so clogged with bodies that it becomes resentful. Though unarmed, it does furious battle with Achilles, squirting him in the eye until he is forced to call for his mother.

Once the river has been tamed, Achilles proceeds to make havoc among the enemy, driving them back to their walls and chasing them into the city, although outnumbered several thousand to one. The long layoff seems to have done him no harm.

Inside Troy, Hector swears he will fight Achilles man to man. His father, King Priam, tries to dissuade him, plucking the gray hairs from his (Priam's) head one by one. His mother, Hecuba, even more dramatically loosens the folds of her robe with one hand and with the other shows Hector her breast, which is meant to remind him of the good old days.

But Hector cannot long be held by such entertainment. Harnessing himself, and taking the bit in his teeth, he fares forth to meet Achilles. However, as soon as he beholds the famous Greek, "brandishing from his right shoulder the Pelian ash," he turns about and "plies swift knees," which is Homer's way of saying he ran like hell.

Plying swift knees

Now it is a race between Achilles fleet of foot and Hector swift of knee, while the gods look down from Olympus and are glad they are not human. Three times Achilles chases the Trojan warrior around the walls of the city until, as Homer says, "Hector's fated day sank down, and fell to the house of Hades," or in other words he was pooped. There was nothing to do but stand and fight.

Achilles throws a spear at Hector and misses, but Athene thoughtfully picks it up and hands it back to him. Yet when Hector's spear bounces off Achilles' shield, no friendly goddess, or even a dog, is around to fetch it for him. This being before the Age of Chivalry, Achilles attacks his unarmed foe, piercing his neck with his ashen spear and thereby bringing an ashen look to Hector's face. But alas, the thrust misses the Trojan's windpipe, an inaccuracy which permits Hector to make two irrelevant speeches before he signs off. After stripping the armor from the corpse in accordance with the thrifty custom of the day,[1] Achilles ties the body to the chariot, feet first, and drags it off through the dust. As Homer says, it is "foul entreatment" of noble Hector, but this is one of the penalties for losing.

There is now a truce between the Trojans and the Greeks, and nothing remains but for both sides to mourn their dead. This the Greeks do by means of chariot races, foot races, boxing and wrestling matches, archery contests, and other shows of sorrow. The Trojans build a huge funeral pyre, burn Hector, and make moan.

To the surprise of most readers, the *Iliad* concludes without any mention of the Wooden Horse or what happened to Achilles' heel. Three almost illegible words at the bottom of the original manuscript, long a puzzle to scholars, have recently been deciphered. They are: "To Be Continued."

[1] In this instance it is his own, though every Tom, Dick, and Hector has been wearing it.

Questions on *The Iliad*

1. Achilles, we are told, sulked in his tent. Wasn't this at least better for the morale of his troops than doing it outside?

2. Which do you think is the chief advantage of being a god:

   a. Being able to take on any shape, especially as you get older?

   b. Looking down on mortals?

3. Thetis is called "the silver-footed." In view of the fact that she was always running around without sandals, could this be a misprint for "the sliver-footed"?

4. How did Dawn get rosy fingers? (Go ahead, make a wild guess.)

5. List the differences if Helen had been carried off to Paris instead of by Paris.

6. Try sleeping on a piece of oxhide, with a shield for a pillow. Now do you see why the Greek warriors always got up in the morning in a fighting mood?

7. If you were Hera and were called "ox-eyed," would you consider it a compliment? What if you were an ox and were called "Hera-eyed"?

8. Since both Patroclus and Hector were killed in Achilles' armor, shouldn't Achilles consider taking his business to another blacksmith?

WILLIAM SHAKESPEARE

William Shakespeare, alias Francis Bacon, Christopher Marlowe, the Earl of Oxford, and the Bard of Avon, was baptized on April 26, 1564. When he was born is disputed, but anyone who argues that it was after this date is just being difficult. Stratford-on-Avon, his birthplace, is situated in what has been described as "gently rolling country," probably by someone who had just got off a ship.

The poet's father, John Shakespeare, is mentioned in contemporary records as a person who cured glove skins, some of which looked pretty sick until he went to work on them. He is said to have been fined 12*d* for failing to remove a pile of dirt from in front of his house. This may seem unimportant to the average reader, but to the scholar who discovered this interesting fact it meant promotion and a substantial increase in salary.

Shakespeare's mother was Mary Arden. Little is recorded about her except that she had eight children and was known for her good breeding.

Our poet's name has been spelled many ways, including Shakspere, Shakespeyre, Shaxpere, Schackspere, and Chacksper, the last of these not even coming close. Shakespeare took all this good-humoredly, but considerable grumbling was heard from the postman.

For a time he was apprenticed to a butcher. All that skewering and hacking, with the blood squirting every which way, made a lasting impression on his young mind. Years later it was faithfully reproduced in the fifth act of each of his tragedies.

When he was eighteen, Shakespeare married Anne Hathaway, whom he courted in the garden of her picturesque cottage in nearby Shottery. Not until too late did he discover that the fragrance that kept him so excited came from the flowers. Anne was eight years older than William, and some scholars believe he became acquainted with her when she was his baby sitter.

Soon after his marriage Shakespeare went into teaching, a career for which he was admirably qualified by having attended the Stratford Grammar School. To support his growing family on his teacher's salary, he worked after hours at odd jobs, such as poaching deer. Anne set a good table, and her poached deer, topped by a poached egg, was a family favorite.

In 1587 or 1588, we are told, Shakespeare "threw down the schoolmaster's rod," apparently disgusted, and went to London. There he found himself in the midst of what was

Willie wooing

known as Pre-Shakespearean Drama. At first, however, he was more interested in sports, particularly swimming, for it is said that "he plunged gladly into the tide of London life and swam strongly with the current." He enjoyed watching people playing at bowls or shooting at butts. The city fascinated him, especially the open sewers where he spent many happy hours sightseeing, and the prison gates "over which grinned the rotting heads of traitors," who were jolly to the last. After all, this was Merrie England.

Suddenly Shakespeare found himself. Where, exactly, is not known, although some think it was in the back room of the Mermaid Tavern, curled up behind a pile of empty ale tankards. At any rate, it was an intense emotional experience, and as soon as he pulled himself together he embarked on his fabulous career. In no time at all he was an actor, a playwright, and part owner of the Globe. But for the discouraging fact that boys took the parts of women, he would also have been a stage-door Johnny. Spectators applauded wildly as he ran from the box office, where he had been checking receipts, and lept onto the stage just in time to resume his part as the lead in one of his plays.

If nothing is known of Shakespeare's home life at this time, it is because he never went home.

Eventually he became quite well-to-do and bought much valuable property. Although his real estate holdings were considerable, it seems an exaggeration to refer, as some scholars do, to "Shakespeare's London." Indeed most of his property was in Stratford, except for a couple of theaters and the factory, stretching for miles along the Thames, known as Shakespeare's Works.

Retiring to Stratford, Shakespeare planted a mulberry tree, from which have come scores of entertaining anecdotes and no telling how many mulberries. He died on April 23, 1616, and his grave is covered with the following inscription in verse which Shakespeare is said to have written himself:

> Good frend for Jesus sake forbeare,
> To digg the dust encloased heare!
> Bleste be the man that spares thes stones,
> And curst be he that moves my bones.

Washington Irving, a man of refinement who was sensitive about such things as spelling and punctuation, has called this "extremely awful." At any rate it has served to keep Shakespeare's bones intact, perhaps by keeping lovers of poetry at a distance.

Kittredge says of *Julius Caesar:* "Phrase after phrase comes straight from North." This may be of interest to those who have trouble with their sense of direction, but actually Shakespeare took the plot and characters from Plutarch's *Lives*, on which, fortunately, the copyright had long since expired.

As for chronology, it is a moot point whether the play was written toward the end of Shakespeare's Second Period or at the beginning of his Third Period. A compromise theory, recently advanced, is that it was written between the two periods, which, if true, will require a drastic and imaginative revision of chronological charts.

Shakespeare's friends were quick to realize that the play was a tragedy, although they were too kind to tell him so. The fact that no contemporary reviews exist fosters the belief that all were bought up and destroyed by Ben Jonson and others to keep Shakespeare from seeing them. It might be of interest to note the modern critical opinion that the central character of *Julius Caesar* is not Julius Caesar but Brutus. As of this writing, however, there is no movement afoot to change the name of the play.

Julius Caesar

The opening scene is in Rome: A Street. A Street is presumably just north of B Street. It is a holiday, the feast of the Lupercalia. This, according to a footnote, was an ancient festival of purification and fertility (an unbeatable combination), when men clad only in goatskins raced around slapping women with goat-hide thongs until they were purified and fertile, or at least black-and-blue. Anyhow, the common people, including a few old goats, are out celebrating the return to Rome of Julius Caesar, who has conquered Pompey.[1]

Flavius and Marullus, two tribunes who are not so en-

[1] Who was soon after assassinated. See *The Last Days of Pompey*.

Two tribunes

thusiastic about Caesar, tell the crowds to stop milling around and blocking traffic. Can't they find some better way of spending their day off, such as watching the lions crunch Christians at the Colosseum, or shouting ribald remarks at the Vestal Virgins?

"What trade art thou?" Marullus asks a cobbler.

"A mender of bad soles," the fellow quips, and Marullus and Flavius are infuriated. Not only is it a bad joke, but they have heard it before.

"You blocks, you stones, you worse than senseless things!" Marullus says to the crowd of commoners, and, considering the passive way they take such epithets, he may be right.

What annoys Flavius is the fact that somebody has draped scarves over a whole row of statues, in honor of Caesar. "Disrobe the images!" he shouts, being a lover of nudes and fearing a wave of puritanism.

Caesar enters, and a soothsayer tries to warn him of something. "Beware the ides of March," the fellow says, but Caesar is unperturbed. The reference is obviously to March 15, which back then was Income Tax Day. Why should he worry? He doesn't pay taxes, he collects them.

Beware the ides. . . .

Caesar then leaves briefly, so that he will not hear two of his followers, Cassius and Brutus, while they talk about him. Cassius tells Brutus that Caesar is getting too big for his toga.

"We petty men walk under his huge legs, and peep about," says Cassius, crouching low in an amusing bit of pantomime. Then he adds, "Upon what meat doth this our Caesar feed, that he is grown so great?" It is probably something that affects the pituitary gland. Cassius, with his "lean and hungry look," is jealous.

Lean and hungry

Caesar now pops in again, staying only long enough to express his distrust of Cassius. "He thinks too much," he confides to his friend Mark Antony who, not guilty of excessive cerebration, is safe to have around.

Caesar has also picked up the odd idea, perhaps from some ill-informed oracle, that skinny men are dangerous, and this is another reason why he distrusts Cassius. "Let me have men about me that are fat," he says. He has in mind roly-poly, good-natured fellows like Falstaff and Hermann Goering.

Caesar, who at this point seems to have little more than a walk-on part, exits again.

That night, as Cassius and the other conspirators plot against Caesar, there is thunder and lightning, lions walk around in the streets, and men go about on fire. These are portents of something, such as unseasonable weather, carelessness on the part of the zoo keeper, or a dangerous increase in incendiarism.

Cassius has no difficulty winning most persons over to his plan to do away with Caesar, but he has to work subtly with Brutus, who is not the sort to murder a close friend without an excuse. The technique Cassius uses is to throw messages through Brutus's window all night. One of these reads: "Brutus, thou sleep'st: awake and see thyself. Shall Rome, &c. Speak, strike, redress."

The message puzzles Brutus. In the first place, how could he possibly sleep, with those cylinders of parchment whizzing in through the window every few minutes? Also the "&c." is ominous, suggesting more than it says. The one thing clear to him is "redress," so he gets up and dons his business toga.

Cassius and the others, disguised to look like Roman conspirators, drop in at dawn. After a night of being peppered with incomprehensible messages, and now receiving guests at dawn, Brutus is in a mood for murder.

"Caesar must bleed for it!" he declares. But Brutus is one who thinks that if a job is worth doing at all it is worth doing well. So he cautions the rest of the gang, who are toying with their daggers, "Let's carve him as a dish fit for the gods, not hew him as a carcass fit for hounds." Warming to the task, he thinks of picking up some paper frills at the butcher shop.

Meanwhile Caesar has had almost as hard a night as

Carve him with care

Brutus. His wife Calpurnia, who talks in her sleep, has been yelling "Help! ho! they murder Caesar!" until his nerves are shot. He arises and paces around, thinking of taking drastic action, such as making his wife sleep in another bedroom.

Calpurnia, seeing him standing by the door in his nightgown, which looks for all the world like a toga, thinks he is about to leave for the Capitol, where he must deal with matters of import.[1] She is unstrung. What a ghastly night, she thinks, even for Rome. The lion that was wandering around downtown had whelped right in the middle of the street, graves had yawned (it was late), and there had been a light drizzle of blood, something not forecast by the weatherman. Calpurnia is not exactly superstitious, but she thinks Caesar should take off his laurel wreath and sandals, relax on the marble sofa, and spend the day looking at his bust collection.[2]

[1] And export as well. The Roman Empire was big business.

[2] The busts are all of himself, but he rather enjoys the monotony.

"You shall not stir out of your house today," says Calpurnia firmly.

"Caesar shall forth," says Caesar, speaking of himself in the third person. It is a habit which he has never been able to break, and his tolerant friends merely wink at each other.

Despite Calpurnia's fears, Caesar insists on getting down to the Capitol. He doesn't want to spoil a perfect attendance record. Besides, his friends will miss him.[1] "Cowards die

You shall not stir

many times before their deaths; the valiant never taste of death but once," he philosophizes. About then that dark-brown taste in his mouth begins to worry him. He decides to stay home, after all, and blame it on his wife.

But when Decius, Ligarius, Metellus, Casca, Trebonius, Cinna, Publius, and Brutus come by and urge him to get to the Capitol without fail, he gives in. Oddly, he does not wonder why eight prominent Romans should come to his

[1] Little does he realize how accurate they are with a dagger at close range.

house so early in the morning and be so insistent that he get to the office. Perhaps they are planning a surprise party for him, and he doesn't want to spoil their fun.

"What is 't o'clock?" he asks.

"Caesar, 't is strucken eight," says Brutus, who, since his native tongue is Latin, may be excused an occasional monstrosity in English. What is less excusable is his saying the clock has struck, when they were using sundials in those days. He may have heard a shadow tapping lightly on the VIII.

As Caesar strides down the street toward the Capitol, a teacher of rhetoric named Artemidorus tries to slip him an essay. It says, in the straightforward if monotonous style which must have been taught in Rhetoric 1: "Caesar, beware of Brutus; take heed of Cassius; come not near Casca; have an eye to Cinna; trust not Trebonius; mark well Metellus Cimber; Decius Brutus loves thee not; thou hast wronged Caius Ligarius." If Caesar had paused to read this little composition, he would have sensed his unpopularity. But, unimpressed by the teacher's "humble suit" amidst all those well-tailored togas, he brushes him aside.

While Caesar stands in front of the Capitol, the conspirators begin to carve him, politely taking turns. Caesar isn't unduly upset, thinking this only about what an officeholder can expect, until he discovers that the last man in the line is his good friend Brutus.

"*Et tu, Brute!*" he exclaims, so astonished that he lapses into Latin.[1] Whereupon, wishing to have the last word, he commands, "Then fall, Caesar!" A disciplined soldier to the end, he salutes himself and drops dead.

[1] Though his words must have baffled the uneducated Elizabethans standing in the pit, Brutus caught on at once. It took some of the zing out of his dagger thrust.

You too?

The conspirators congratulate themselves, believing they have saved Rome from tyranny. Perhaps they have, perhaps not. But they *have* set a precedent for palace revolutions for the next two thousand years.

Before leaving the scene of the murder, Brutus has a gruesome idea. "Let us bathe our hands in Caesar's blood up to the elbows," he suggests, "and besmear our swords." For mystery story readers this is a welcome change from the way murderers usually try to remove all traces of blood and obliterate fingerprints. Brutus likes to be different.

While they are rinsing off with Caesar's blood, Antony happens by.

"O mighty Caesar! dost thou lie so low?" he asks the body, without any real expectation of an answer. Then, never having been carved before, except in marble, he begs the murderers to do the same to him. But they decline, so weary from stabbing that they can hardly lift their daggers. Some other day, perhaps. Each of them, however, will give him a bloody handshake; if he gets any pleasure out of this he's welcome to it.

After the others leave, Antony stays to prepare the body. Unlike the modern mortician, he does this by talking to it. But his monologue is by popular request, for Caesar's wounds, as Antony says, "like dumb mouths do ope their ruby lips to beg the voice and utterance of my tongue."

Shortly afterward, at the Forum, Brutus addresses the plebeians, neatly explaining why he killed Caesar. "Not that I loved Caesar less," he says, "but that I loved Rome more." His audience, impressed by such a beautifully constructed sentence in an extemporaneous speech, bursts into applause. After working in a few congratulatory references to Romulus and Remus, he concludes with a mention of Jove. Then he leads the crowd in the Pledge of Allegiance to Senatus Populusque Romanus. It is the ideal political speech.

With the applause ringing in his ears, Brutus heads for the men's room to get that blood off his hands.

Mark Antony

And now Antony has the floor. Glad at last to be playing to a live audience, he plunges into what is known as Mark Antony's Famous Speech.

"Friends, Romans, countrymen, lend me your ears," he begins, getting a laugh at the very start. "I come to bury Caesar, not to praise him," he promises, and then forgets his promise completely. It is a superlative speech. Indeed, in referring to Brutus's stabbing of Caesar as "the most unkindest cut of all," it is doubly superlative. The effect of the speech is to cause the fickle rabble, who a few minutes before had thought Brutus was simply great, to chase him out of town. Seldom has a rabble rouser roused a rabble so effectively. Antony has a bright career ahead of him in the Roman Senate.

He now joins with two other leaders, Octavius and Lepidus, to wage war against the murderers of Caesar. If they win, they will rule Rome as a triumvirate, a system of government which assumes that three heads are better than

The triumvirs

one.[1] It is also a system whereby if any one of the three steps out of the room, the other two say uncomplimentary things about him, which is what happens almost immediately to Lepidus.

In the enemy camp, Brutus and Cassius meet in Brutus's tent to plan the crucial battle, which is to be fought at Philippi in 42 B.C. for historical reasons. The two leaders have a falling out over military matters, as is characteristic of any Allied High Command, and Cassius spiritedly asserts that he is a better soldier than Brutus.

"You are not," says Brutus.

"I am," says Cassius.

"I say you are not," says Brutus.

While this exciting interchange continues, full of the stuff of poetry, high drama, and field marshals' memoirs, the Battle of Philippi must wait. Finally Cassius hands Brutus a dagger, bares his breast, and in a moment of extreme generosity invites him to take out his heart. It is a gift with no strings, though perhaps a few arteries, attached. But Brutus declines.

"Sheathe your dagger," he says. Some sources claim that he added, "and button up your tunic. You're out of uniform."

Now there seems to be nothing left to attack but the enemy. "There is a tide in the affairs of men," says Brutus, "which taken at the flood leads on to fortune." This has proved splendid counsel, down the centuries, for those who can swim.

That night Brutus goes to bed early, wanting to get his eight hours before the big battle on the morrow. While he is reading, the ghost of Caesar seeps in. At first Brutus

[1] So long as they are not all on one body.

Caesar seeps in

fails to recognize his old friend, who has changed considerably. Gone is the puffiness under the eyes, the Caesar-size paunch.

"Ha!" he laughs, "who comes here . . . that mak'st my blood cold and my hairs to stare?" Peeking out through his follicles, he naturally has difficulty being sure who it is. The ghost of Caesar, not nearly so talkative as the ghost of Hamlet's dad, exits after three brief sentences, and it seems hardly worth his while to have come.

The next day, on the plains of Philippi, the opposing armies are met.[1] The leaders of the two forces have a parley, which means that they assemble in No Man's Land and trade insults. "Words before blows," says Brutus, knowing that some of the participants won't be around to talk after the battle.

Just before the parley breaks up, Octavius remarks wryly

[1] By whom, it is never divulged.

to Brutus and Cassius, "If you dare fight today, come to the field; if not, when you have stomachs." They need stomachs to buckle their armor onto.

The battle lasts only a couple of hundred lines. Cassius, receiving a false report that his friend Titinius has been surrounded by the enemy, is ready to call it quits. He is as lean and hungry as ever, but not so dangerous. It being too awkward to stab himself with his sword, he orders his servant, Pindarus, to do it. Pindarus obediently follows through,[1] not realizing until later that he has done himself out of a job.

Titinius, returning to find Cassius dead, is overcome by empathy and kills himself with Cassius' sword. This is the very weapon that Cassius poked through Caesar, a few acts ago, and one shudders at how unsanitary it is for everybody to be using it.

Moments later, finding Cassius dead and realizing that the battle is lost, Brutus, too, has the self-destructive urge. Unlike Cassius, he insists on at least partly doing it himself. So he asks his friends if one of them won't please be a good fellow and hold his sword out for him to run at. But each in turn excuses himself, saying his hand is a little unsteady. It would be embarrassing if Brutus were to run at a wobbly sword and miss it completely.

Finally Brutus persuades his servant, Strato, to hold the sword for him. "And turn away thy face," he says thoughtfully, thinking it better to turn the fellow's face than his stomach. Then he backs off a few paces and comes running. You have to admire the man's nerve, though there must have been some easier way.

Antony is really sorry that Brutus ever got mixed up with

[1] Slicing a little.

Strato holds the sword

the conspirators and came to such a regrettable end. "This was the noblest Roman of them all," he asserts, forgetting what he said about Caesar in his funeral oration. Then he adds what would seem to be obvious, to wit, "This was a man."

Octavius tells them where to stow the body of Brutus. "Within my tent his bones tonight shall lie," he says hospitably. Then, in a festive mood, he suggests a little celebration, putting his invitation into rhyme:

> "So call the field to rest, and let's away,
> To part the glories of this happy day."

It *has* been a happy day, for those who are still alive. For the others, who knows? A clue may be found in the final words, "*Exeunt omnes*," which may be freely translated, "Everybody has to go sometime."

Questions on *Julius Caesar*

1. In Shakespeare's plays have you noticed how soothsayers always say the sooth, the whole sooth, and nothing but the sooth?

2. Have you a lean and hungry friend who thinks too much? If so, he is probably thinking about food.

3. If a lion in the street seems ominous, think of one on the sidewalk.

4. When the conspirators stop at Caesar's house at 8 A.M. and invite him to go to the Capitol with them, could it be because he belongs to their chariot pool?

5. Isn't it a pity that Calpurnia, having warned Caesar not to go out on the ides of March, never has a chance to say to him, "I told you so"?

6. When Brutus washed his hands in the blood of the murdered Caesar, wasn't he making a bloody fool of himself?

7. "My heart is in the coffin there with Caesar," says Mark Antony during his famous funeral oration, "and I must pause till it come back to me." Couldn't he just have been out of breath?

8. When you read that Antony's army was quartered at Sardis, don't let it worry you. Wasn't Brutus's army decimated at Philippi?

9. Would Brutus have been quite so casual about seeing the ghost of Caesar if he had read *Hamlet* and *Macbeth?*

SIR WALTER SCOTT

Scott was a Scot. As a boy, he was a boy Scot. He was proud of his ancestry, which included William Scott, who was captured by one Gideon Murray [1] and given the choice of marrying Murray's ugliest daughter or being hanged. To the eternal shame (and possibly disfigurement) of the Scotts, he passed up the gallows.

Scott's mother, we are told, had ten bairns. An indefatigable woman, she also found time to have a child, Walter, who was born in Edinburgh on August 15, 1771. According to Lockhart,[2] whose seven-volume life of Scott

[1] Surely there were not two Gideon Murrays.

[2] Scott's son-in-law. A hint to contemporary biographers who are having trouble getting access to the private papers of their subjects.

gives us at least the essentials, Walter as a small boy was "an incomparable story teller," but he seems not to have been punished by his indulgent parents. They were grateful that he was not a drunk and a woman chaser like Bobby Burns, who lived to be only thirty-seven and had to make every minute count.

Soon Scott became interested in collecting ballads of the Border, about such heroic exploits as getting past English customs officials without paying duty. On his ballad-collecting expeditions he suffered many discomforts, one biographer relating that "he was often compelled to sleep on the same straw with his horse."

Subsequently Scott studied law and wrote a thesis on the disposal of the dead bodies of criminals. It was voted the most gruesome thesis of the year. There is no evidence, however, that he pursued this specialty after he became a barrister.

To pick up some money on the side, Scott became sheriff of Selkirkshire. Being a sheriff in the Far North is easier

Sheriff Scott

than being a sheriff in the Far West, and he never had to shoot it out with any Scottish bad men. Somehow it is hard to imagine Scott with a handlebar mustache, a big shiny star, and a reputation for being quick on the draw.

For Scott was a gentle gentleman, rarely mean of mien, who wore a large cravat and the highest collar until Herbert Hoover. His moral standards were not only irreproachable but unapproachable, and he loved such simple pleasures as sitting by the hearth with a good book, sound asleep.

Scott's literary career began with the great success of a long poem, *The Lay of the Last Minstrel,* which everybody read to find out where and whom. If they were looking for something naughty, they were sadly disappointed. Scott intended to follow this with *The Lay of the Land* and others, but after *The Lay of the Lake* decided to lay off. In plain truth he was forced out of the poetry business by Byron, who was more exotic, erotic, and erratic.[1] Scott, having a lot of paper[2] and ink left over, went into novel writing.

His first fat volumes were called the Waverley Novels, which, as the name indicates, were somewhat unsteady of aim. Scott considered them potboilers, and so did those readers who used them to keep the fire in the cookstove going when they ran out of coal. He did not put his name on them, and people tried to pretend they had no idea who was the author. However, his books brought him fame and fortune, and he began to be called Sir Walter and to sign his name Walter Scott, Bart.[3]

Scott bought a country place called Abbotsford, because,

[1] See his childish misspelling of "child" in *Childe Harold.*

[2] The original Scott Tissue.

[3] Which led some to believe that he had become a bartender.

as he said, "I wished to settle myself where I could spit in the Tweed." People who came to call on him were well advised to approach the house under an umbrella. With the money he made from his books, Scott bought more and more land around Abbotsford, until his property stretched for miles and at many points he was out of range of the Tweed. According to an admiring biographer, the house itself, a magnificent pile, was "built with his pen," which is hard to believe.

What caused him to discontinue acquiring real estate was the fact that his publisher went bankrupt. This would be distressing to any author, but Scott had an additional reason to be upset. He owned the publishing house. At least he was a silent partner, and only regretted not occasionally having said something, such as "No."

A man of integrity as well as industry, Scott decided to write his way out of debt. Clearing a small space amongst the bills, he began turning out novels so fast that he is suspected of having used an electric typewriter. Sometimes he thought out a whole novel while riding at a gallop through the braes, and was sorry that his horse was unable to take dictation.

Try as he might, however, he could not pay all he owed during his lifetime. When he died, in 1832, his funeral was attended by an unusually large crowd of creditors who sincerely mourned his passing.

Ivanhoe

The story is set in the time of Richard Coeur-de-Lion, who has been away from England on a crusade for so long that he is beloved by everyone. Everyone, that is, but Prince John, who has been trying on the crown for size, and some of his henchmen, such as Reginald Front-de-Boeuf (or Beef-Head), who will lose their jobs if Richard returns. These are the days of chivalry, when people are very courteous about the way they hit each other over the head with staves and run each other through with spears. They would never think of shooting anyone, because gunpowder has not yet been invented.

Prince John

It is only a few generations after the Norman Conquest, and the Normans and Saxons, who are inclined to bear a grudge, are still mad at each other. In fact, since the Normans use French and the Saxons use Anglo-Saxon, they are not on speaking terms. Both the Normans and the Saxons look down on the Jews, which is very Christian of them.

At the beginning of the story we meet Gurth, a swineherd, and Wamba, a jester, who are enthralled by [1] Cedric of Rotherwood, a Saxon. Wamba, being the son of Witless, comes by his low IQ naturally. While they are out tending Cedric's swine, a monk and a knight and their retinue come riding up and ask the whereabouts of an inn, hostel, or flophouse, where they may spend the night.

"If the reverend fathers loved good cheer and soft lodging," says Wamba, "few miles of riding would carry them to the Priory of Brinxworth, where their quality could not but secure them the most honorable reception; or if they preferred spending a penitential evening, they might turn down yonder wild glade, which would bring them to the hermitage of Copmanhurst, where a pious anchoret would make them sharers for the night of the shelter of his roof and the benefit of his prayers." Wamba may be short-witted, but he is long-winded.

The monk, Prior Aylmer, and the knight, Brian de Bois-Guilbert, wind up spending the night as guests of Cedric the Saxon in his mansion with dirt floors.[2] Cedric himself is a surly fellow who takes his sword and spear to the dinner table and is likely to cut your hand off if you reach for the crust he has his eyes on. But, though he hates Normans, he

[1] I.e., thralls of. They don't really care for him.

[2] A sensible feature. Dirt floors absorb the beef drippings and never have to be mopped or waxed.

is willing to share with his guests his meager fare of swine's flesh, fowl, deer, goats, hares,[1] fish, loaves of bread, fruit, honey, mead, and wine. All he asks in return is an occasional belch of contentment.

Cedric's ward is the beautiful Lady Rowena, a flaxen-haired Saxon who, Scott reports blushingly, is "formed in the best proportions of her sex." They are just starting to eat dinner when Rowena comes in, and Brian de Bois-Guilbert chokes on a shank of venison. Rowena is well swathed in her robe and kirtle, but one wrist is bare, and the sight of this expanse of flesh undoes the knight. He has been in Palestine so long that he has forgotten what a blonde looks like. "Yoiks!" he croaks, breaking out in a cold sweat.

But Rowena snubs Bois-Guilbert, and pulls up her veil so that he gets not even a titillating glimpse of her shell-like

[1] Each guest may have a whole one. Cedric is no hare-splitter.

He had forgotten about blondes

ears. There is to be a tourney on the morrow, at Ashby-de-la-Zouche, and Rowena wishes Ivanhoe were back from his crusade with Richard. She knows he could unhorse Bois-Guilbert with a lance made of peanut brittle. But Bois-Guilbert loudly proclaims that he isn't afraid of Ivanhoe, who presumably is several thousand miles away and anyhow hasn't sent in his entry fee for the tournament.

Among those who spend the night at Cedric's mansion, which is taking on the proportions of a railway station, are a humble palmer [1] and a Jewish moneylender by the name of Isaac. Isaac stakes the palmer, under whose weeds he perceives the flower of knighthood, to horses and equipment to enter the tournament at Ashby.

Everybody is at the tournament, from Prince John to Isaac the moneylender and his daughter Rebecca. Scott, who would fain omit no detail, gives a page to "the brilliancy of her eyes, the superb arch of her eyebrows, her well-

[1] A pilgrim who has made it all the way to the Holy Land and lived to tell the tale, over and over.

formed aquiline nose, her teeth as white as pearl, her profusion of sable tresses," etc. Indeed he goes a little far in saying that the three uppermost clasps of her vest "were left unfastened on account of the heat, which . . . enlarged the prospect to which we allude." (For shame, Sir Walter!)

The first day of the tournament there is much sounding of trumpets, waving of handkerchiefs, and derring-do. Knights ride hell-bent across the field and try to unhorse one another, splintering lances, denting armor, and loosening teeth. Havoc is wreaked by an unknown champion, calling himself the Disinherited Knight, who unhorses Bois-Guilbert, unhelmets Sir Philip Malvoisin, unnerves De Grantmesnil, and gives Ralph de Vipont a bloody nose. Prince John acclaims him the victor, with the right to select the Queen of Beauty and of Love, broadly hinting that a good choice would be Alicia, the daughter of Waldemar Fitzurse. But the unknown knight selects the Lady Rowena, and Prince John is pleased not a whit.

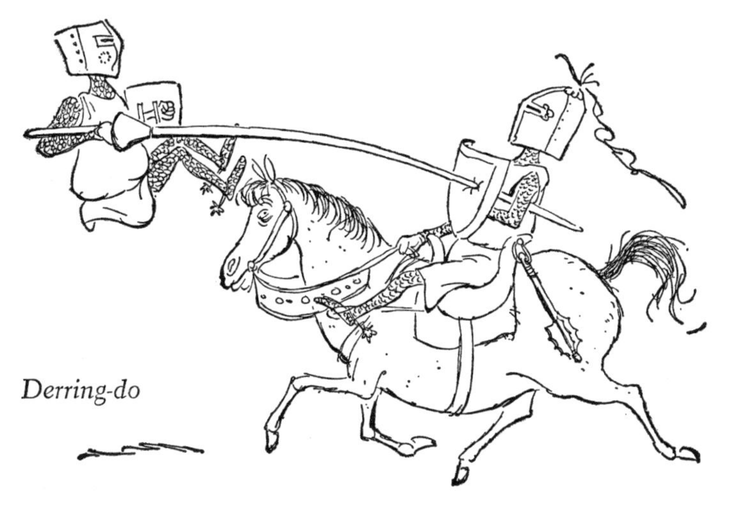

Derring-do

The second day of the tournament, before a sellout crowd, the Disinherited Knight is about to get the better of Bois-Guilbert again when two bruisers, Front-de-Boeuf and Athelstane, come to Bois-Guilbert's assistance, and the three of them gang up on the Disinherited Knight. (There are many rules in medieval jousting, but there is little sportsmanship.) Just as he is about to be massacred, a powerful knight dressed all in black appears from Nowhere and in a trice has the Disinherited Knight's opponents on the ground. Then he rides off nonchalantly before he can be given a guerdon or even a cool drink.

The Disinherited Knight, however, swoons from a wound, and when they remove his helmet they discover that he is Ivanhoe! [1] It now comes out that Ivanhoe is the son of Cedric the Saxon and lover of Rowena. He has been disinherited and sent away by his father, who hopes by the marriage of Rowena and Athelstane (an oaf whom Rowena detests) to restore a Saxon to the throne of England. As a matchmaker and a father, Cedric leaves much to be desired.

Prince John is sore annoyed at the thought that Ivanhoe has returned, for he has given Ivanhoe's fief to Front-de-Boeuf, and a fief is no easy thing to get back, God wot. "His wounds must be looked into," says Prince John, apparently solicitous of the injured Ivanhoe. Then he adds, "Our own physician shall attend him." As he speaks, an evil smile curls the prince's lip, and you have the feeling that this particular physician is one whose patients rarely pull through.

But Ivanhoe has disappeared, leaving behind him only a small spot of blood, and Prince John, he of the curled lip, is foiled.

[1] Whose first name, let it be said and then forgotten, is Wilfred.

The prince is also vexed when, in the archery contest, his favorite archer is defeated by an unknown churl named Locksley. Locksley, who is obviously someone famous in disguise,[1] hits the bull's-eye without half aiming, and then slams an arrow through a willow wand about as thick as a man's thumb.[2]

Shortly after the tournament, Cedric the Saxon, Athelstane, Rowena, and their entourage are cautiously making their way through the woods, which are full of outlaws. Suddenly they are set upon by a band of Normans led by Maurice de Bracy and Brian de Bois-Guilbert, and carried off to the castle of Front-de-Boeuf. Also captured are Isaac

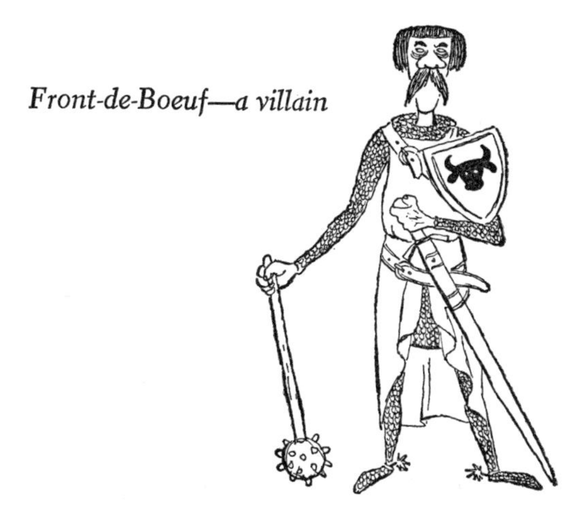

Front-de-Boeuf—a villain

and his daughter Rebecca, who are likewise passing through the woods at the moment, with the wounded Ivanhoe in a litter.[3] It is hard to see the forest for the people.

[1] Annie Oakley, probably.

[2] True, men's thumbs were a little thicker in those days.

[3] Apparently they do not notice the signs, posted everywhere, saying "No Litter."

In Front-de-Boeuf's castle, a forbidding place with a moat, drawbridge, portcullis, turret, and other features discouraging to door-to-door salesmen, the prisoners are cordially mistreated. Each is assigned to a private bedroom with connecting dungeon. Front-de-Boeuf, with the assistance of two muscular Saracen slaves, threatens to roast Isaac betimes on a charcoal grill if he will not pay a thousand pounds of silver forthwith. Since he doesn't have that much with him, indeed couldn't lift that much, it appears to be a question only of whether he will come out of the experience rare, medium, or well done.

In another part of the castle, De Bracy, dressed in his best doublet and carrying a sword from which all traces of blood have been carefully removed, bursts into Rowena's apartment and asks for her hand. Rowena, who knows this is not all he wants, proudly rejects him, even though he threatens to torture Ivanhoe and Cedric on the rack, mayhap squeezing their heads with knotted cords. This may not be the best way to win a woman's affection or to insure a happy marriage, but De Bracy believes in the direct approach.

Meanwhile, in still another of the castle's apartments, Bois-Guilbert is wooing Rebecca with even less subtlety. Being a Christian knight with high ideals, Bois-Guilbert contemplates nothing so demeaning as marrying the Jewess. He has in mind a less permanent attachment, such as rape.[1] But Rebecca finds the man quite unattractive, as she hints when she threatens to jump from the window.

The dastardly Front-de-Boeuf and his dastardly friends are interrupted in their dastardly pursuits by the sound of

[1] Scott calls Bois-Guilbert "an unprincipled voluptuary," which is hard to improve on.

Wooing Rebecca

someone winding a horn (Scott's horns always seem to be running down) in the nearby forest. Marry, the castle is surrounded by an army of outlaws and Saxons led by Locksley (who is really Robin Hood), the Black Knight (who is really King Richard), and Wamba (who is really Wamba). "Curses!" says Front-de-Boeuf in twelfth-century French.

To spy on the Normans, the outlaws send Wamba, dressed in priest's garb, into the castle. There, setting a precedent for Sydney Carton in *A Tale of Two Cities*, he changes clothes with Cedric the Saxon, sacrificing his freedom but improving his attire. Eftsoons, or as soon as he is able to swallow his pride, which goes down pretty easily, Cedric heads for the nearest exit. On the way out he meets Urfried, a hag who in her better days was the beautiful daughter of Torquil Wolfganger.

"Thou the daughter of Torquil Wolfganger!" [1] exclaims Cedric. Torquil was a noble Saxon who had been his father's best friend. Urfried, it seems, was the mistress of Front-de-Boeuf's father, a lecherous fellow whom Front-de-Boeuf

[1] He had forgotten the face but not the name.

killed in a reckless moment of parricide. Now, with most of her teeth missing, her once-creamy complexion curdled, and her grizzled hair a mess, she is no longer the darling of the Normans, and she is bitter about it. Remembering that she is a Saxon,[1] she promises to help in the assault on the castle. Her contribution will be to make a face and scare hell out of the defenders.

But we must retrace our steps, as Scott does every other chapter, to see what has happened to Ivanhoe. Or, in Scott's words: "Our history must needs retrograde for the space of a few pages, to inform the reader of certain passages material to his understanding of the rest of this important narrative." It was Rebecca who was responsible for rescuing Ivanhoe after the tournament at Ashby, and she now tends him as he lies wounded in Front-de-Boeuf's castle. She is not only beautiful but a Registered Nurse, and Ivanhoe is in good hands. Indeed, though he is faithful to Rowena, it is odd how madly his heart pounds when Rebecca takes his pulse.

The siege of the castle continues unabated. Front-de-Boeuf is struck down by the Black Knight and on his death-

[1] A bit tardily, methinks.

Rebecca takes Ivanhoe's pulse

bed is given a lecture by the vengeful Urfried, who consigns his soul to hell, special delivery. Then she sets fire to his apartment so that he will get a foretaste of what is in store for him.

As flames lap the castle, a mighty assault is made over barbican, moat, postern, and sally port, using pavises, pikestaffs, and halberds. (Scott makes it sound as medieval as all get out.) The defenders are overcome, and Ivanhoe is rescued from the flames by the Black Knight. But Bois-Guilbert, as unprincipled a voluptuary as ever, sneaks in, disguised as a fire chief, and carries off Rebecca.

Athelstane, thinking it is Rowena who is being abducted,

Athelstane

puts up a fight with Bois-Guilbert. But Bois-Guilbert, dropping the Saxon to the ground with a mighty sword stroke, leaves him for dead. Then he gallops off with Rebecca, panting more from passion than from exertion.

The castle is full of smoke and the floors are slippery with blood, yet Cedric, Rowena, and the others manage to slosh down the corridors to safety. Only Urfried remains atop a turret until it collapses with her, meanwhile chanting the strophes of a barbarous hymn. What with the din of battle and a general distaste for poetry, nobody is listening.

Isaac, rescued with the others from the flaming castle, now bestirs himself to ransom Rebecca from her abductor, Bois-Guilbert, who has carried her off to the preceptory of Templestowe, a kind of YMCA. He appeals to the Grand Master of the order, Lucas Beaumanoir, a spoilsport who does not look with favor on keeping a beautiful young Jewess in the men's dormitory. But Beaumanoir brilliantly concludes that Rebecca must be a sorceress who has cast a spell over Bois-Guilbert. Why else would the man have brought her into the preceptory and established her in an adjoining apartment? (The Grand Master is advanced in age.)

Rebecca, sweet and forgiving through it all, is tried for witchcraft. Damning evidence against her comes from a Saxon peasant with the mellifluous name of Higg, son of Snell. It seems that Rebecca once cured him of the palsy with some homemade balsam, and she is therefore either a necromancer or the owner of a do-it-yourself pharmacopoeia. She is sentenced to death at the stake unless she finds a stalwart champion who can defeat Bois-Guilbert in single combat. In medieval justice, possession of a strong right arm is nine points of the law.

Bois-Guilbert, who is not all bad (though mostly), hates to doom the innocent Rebecca by killing her champion. As he says, speaking with the modesty that becomes a Knight Templar, he can defeat anyone but (1) King Richard, who (he thinks!) is in a faraway prison, and (2) Ivanhoe, who is still weak from his wounds. "If I appear in the lists," says Bois-Guilbert to Rebecca, "thou diest by the stake and faggot," obviously not a pleasant way to go. He suggests that they run off together to Palestine and start life afresh. For her sake he would renounce knighthood and take up a new career, perhaps as a tourist guide. But she politely refuses, a short life at the stake seeming preferable. Bois-Guilbert, beginning to feel unwanted, takes a long look at himself in the mirror.

Returning to the Black Knight, we find him riding through the woods,[1] when he is pounced upon by a band of ruffians. Though he lays about him with his sword and kills a knave, a churl, a seneschal, or a caitiff with each stroke, they are too many for him, and he is nigh to being overcome. Luckily, bethinking himself of the bugle given him by Locksley, he sounds a mot, whereupon Locksley and his men spring out of the woods, where they are always within bugle mot, and soon bestrew the ground with the bodies of the Black Knight's assailants. Their leader, it is disclosed when his visor is lifted,[2] is none other than Waldemar Fitzurse, acting on the orders of Prince John! John will do anything, short of holding a general election, to keep Richard from the throne.

Now (and it is about time) the Black Knight reveals himself as Richard Coeur-de-Lion, which is a great surprise to Locksley, and Locksley reveals himself as Robin Hood, which is a great surprise to Richard. It is probably the most revealing and surprising scene in the book. But the reader, having been tipped off a couple of hundred pages back, may be forgiven a certain smugness.

Everyone now goes to the castle of Cedric the Saxon,

[1] A sure indication of impending disaster, as anyone but Scott's characters should know by now.

[2] This always seems an invasion of privacy.

The Black Knight reveals himself

who is staging the Funeral of the Year for poor Athelstane. There is such feasting and drinking as will no doubt cause additional deaths, followed by additional funeral festivities. Certes, these were parlous times. But the funeral takes a happy, or at least unexpected, turn. Athelstane suddenly staggers in, dressed in his burial garments. By the holy rood, he is not dead, after all! Seems he was only accidentally buried, as he insists on telling the mourners. They listen politely, though the fun has now gone out of the party. Dead or alive, Athelstane is a bore.

Thanks to the intercession of King Richard, Cedric forgives Ivanhoe (who never did anything wrong) and dis-disinherits him. Since Athelstane at last realizes that Rowena will never be his, he generously says Ivanhoe can have her. But for the unhappy plight of Rebecca, whom we had almost forgotten, the book could at this point come to an end.

"Our scene," says Scott, "now returns to the exterior of

the castle, or preceptory, of Templestowe," and not a minute too soon. Rebecca is at the stake, and unless a champion is found to meet Bois-Guilbert, she will shortly go up in smoke. At the last moment, up rides Ivanhoe. Out of breath though he is, he is able to blurt out a few words to explain his presence.

"I am a good knight and noble," he says modestly, "come hither to sustain with lance and sword the just and lawful quarrel of this damsel, Rebecca, daughter of Isaac of York; to uphold the doom pronounced against her to be false and truthless, and to defy Sir Brian de Bois-Guilbert as a traitor, murderer, and liar; as I will prove in this field with my body against his, by the aid of God, of Our Lady, and of Monseigneur St. George, the good knight." With the words "good knight" he makes it clear that he has finished, and many expect him to bow politely and go home to bed. But he waits only a moment for applause [1] before plunging into combat.

[1] It *was* a good speech, wasn't it? Either Ivanhoe had memorized it or he spoke from notes.

I am a good knight

Ivanhoe and Bois-Guilbert ride at each other full tilt. His horse weary and he himself not fully recovered from his wounds, Ivanhoe goes down at the first touch of Bois-Guilbert's lance. But, though Ivanhoe barely grazes him with his shield, Bois-Guilbert goes down too. Spectators who have money on the contest begin to grumble that B-G. has taken a dive. However, when Ivanhoe springs at the fallen knight with his sword, his foe is found to be—dead! "Unscathed by the lance of his enemy, he had died a victim of his own contending passions." Psychosomatic trauma? A broken heart? Indigestion? Whatever it was, it leaves Ivanhoe, sword in hand, looking foolish.

Rebecca is deemed innocent. King Richard reclaims his throne.[1] Ivanhoe marries Rowena. The Normans and Saxons cease their enmity. Scott is well into his next novel.

Marry, for the reader who has not had enow, there are still the Notes and the Glossary.

[1] With a new seat cover and some gilt paint, a reclaimed throne looks as good as new.

Questions on *Ivanhoe*

1. With conditions as they were in England in the twelfth century, do you blame King Richard for always going on crusades?

2. Did you ever hear about the king of the beasts that was called Lion the Richard-hearted?

3. Reference is made to "the polished arms of the knights." Is this because they waxed too enthusiastic?

4. If you saw a man dressed all in green, would you think he was:

   a. An Irishman on St. Patrick's Day?
   b. Camouflaged?
   c. Fond of the color, but overdoing it?

5. Compare trial by combat with trial by jury, and then try to keep out of trouble.

6. Scott tells us that Brian de Bois-Guilbert's eyes could be seen burning like coals, even though his visor was down. Might he have been smoking a cigar? Two cigars?

7. Do you consider the resuscitation of Athelstane improbable, or merely unfortunate?

8. Honestly, how could Ivanhoe have picked that dumb blonde, Rowena, over Rebecca?

NATHANIEL HAWTHORNE

Nathaniel Hawthorne was born in Salem, Massachusetts on July 4, 1804, and it was probably the fright he received from the firecrackers and pinwheels that caused him to become so shy and withdrawn the rest of his life. The name was originally Hathorne, but one day, when he was just fooling around, he inserted the "w" and, try as he might, could never pry it out again. The rest of the family plodded along with the name Hathorne and looked upon Nathaniel as a typographical error.

Among Hawthorne's American ancestors was a magistrate who ordered the whipping of a Quakeress, and a judge who presided over the Salem witch trials. They thought they were only doing their duty, but Hawthorne thought they were overdoing it. He referred to them as his "sable-cloaked, steeple-crowned progenitors," and thought they had bats in their hats.[1] Although it was now a hundred and fifty years since they had been so mean, Hawthorne still felt just sick about it.

Salem had earlier been a busy shipping center, but when our author lived there it was a sleepy seaport, where people went around yawning all day. They had even stopped persecuting witches by the time Hawthorne was a boy. The town was dead.

His father, a sea captain, died early, and Nathaniel was brought up by his mother in what was known as "genteel poverty," which meant that even when hungry he never let his stomach rumble. His clothes might be threadbare, but the holes were evenly spaced and symmetrical. The household was "infected with gloom," which in those days was incurable, and if Nat ever heard laughter, it came from a house down the street.

At seventeen he went to Bowdoin, which was then, his biographer states, "a raw little school in Maine," a condition which must have made a sensitive young man like Hawthorne shudder. After college, he worked for a time in the Boston Custom House, where he was a measurer of coal and salt. Measuring coal was a grimy business at best, but it was figuring out the length and breadth of grain after grain of salt that all but ruined his eyesight.

Next he tried Brook Farm, which was full of Transcendentalists who could see right through material things, such as doors and walls, and gave a man no privacy. The

[1] Considered less embarrassing, at least by Puritans, than having ants in their pants.

Transcendentalists

idea in this Utopian community, where dwelt bearded men and bony, argumentive women, was that people should work with their hands and think.[1] After a hard day in the fields they came home to their communal living, passing around the one cake of soap and spending the evening in reverie, which was a high-class stupor.

Hawthorne fell in love with Sophia Peabody, an intellectual who had a cute set of ideas. Not wanting to share her with the Transcendentalists, he married her and took her to live in the Old Manse, in Concord. The collection of stories he wrote there he called *Mosses from an Old Manse,* not realizing how many botanists would be misled.

This being before the day when a writer could be supported by a Guggenheim, a Rockefeller, or a Fulbright, and there being no summer writers' conferences, Hawthorne

[1] With their heads.

was forced to go to work. The blow was cushioned somewhat by his becoming a government employee. He took a post as Surveyor of the Port of Salem, a position which required him to sit on his front porch and look out over the harbor. The appointment was made by the Democratic administration of James K. Polk, Hawthorne apparently having done well on the qualifying examination, which consisted of a single searching question: "Are you a Democrat?" His loss of the job, when the Whigs came to power, made him so gloomy that he wrote *The Scarlet Letter*.[1]

Hawthorne held one other position, that of United States consul in Liverpool. This appointment came directly from President Franklin Pierce, who had been a fellow student of Hawthorne's at Bowdoin, and wore the same old school cravat.

Seldom in the public eye, Hawthorne lived quietly with his family in houses like the Old Manse and The Wayside, although Malcolm Cowley tells us that in 1837 "he was trying to escape from his owl's nest." This is the only evidence we have that he once lived with the birds and found the experience not wholly satisfactory.[2]

With his large brow, drooping mustache, and drooping spirits, Hawthorne was coming more and more to look like Edgar Allan Poe. He was definitely a Romantic, for he liked to muse in the moonlight or by a dim coal fire when, he says, "ghosts might enter here, without affrighting us." In fact he considered an evening lost when a few ghosts did not drop in.

All the time Hawthorne kept writing. Among the works

[1] You can never tell what a man disappointed by politics will do.

[2] Hawthorne is also said to have "dwelt over-much with shadows." He seems to have preferred almost anything to people.

he produced were *The House of the Seven Gables,* about the Gable family, a collection of old jokes called *Twice-Told Tales,* and *A Wonder Book,* which is for children, or at least not against them.

Hawthorne was fascinated by the grim Puritan past and believed in original sin. Even when it was unoriginal and imitative he found it rather interesting. Yet there was a great deal of New England decorum and prudery in Hawthorne's make-up. For instance, he thought nude paintings were disgusting. Nevertheless, two of his four novels deal with adultery, and some of his characters go in for incest and fratricide. The reason for this apparent inconsistency may be, as one critic says, that there were two Hawthornes.

If so, both of them died on May 19, 1864.

The Scarlet Letter

The story is set in Boston, back in colonial times, when sin was really sinful. Everyone there is a Puritan, since all the other people are either still in England or have gone to Virginia or to hell. The Puritans are a gloomy lot, and by the time the reader gets to the second paragraph, in which the author dwells lovingly on jails and cemeteries, he knows this is no place to be looking for laughs.

As the narrative begins, a crowd has gathered in front of the weather-stained prison door. Growing by the door is a rosebush, and the reader who is alert to such things knows

A gloomy lot

it is a Symbol. Nevertheless, just to be sure, Hawthorne picks one of the roses and explains that this will serve "to symbolize some sweet moral blossom" which, he says, will "relieve the darkening close of a tale of human frailty and sorrow." Hawthorne then presents the rose to the reader, who can either clutch it nervously in his hand while he reads or press it in the book if it is not a library copy.

At last the door of the jail opens, and out comes Hester Prynne, a tall young woman "with a figure of perfect elegance on a large scale." The women among the spectators, all of whom wear petticoats and farthingales and have noses sharp enough to use for letter openers, whisper to each other, hoping Hester can hear. In their humble opinion she is a naughty baggage, a malefactress, and a transgressoress.

What fascinates the onlookers is something embroidered on Hester's bosom or, more accurately, on her dress. It is not only embroidered but illuminated, so that it will be visible by night. This ornament is a SCARLET LETTER. The letter, which the prisoner has fashioned herself with a needle friends smuggled to her in a pincushion, is an "A." Apparently she had intended to go through the alphabet, making a New England sampler, but ran out of thread.

Hester and her A

Prodded along by a grim beadle, Hester makes her way to the market place, where she climbs up onto the scaffold, without, however, "undergoing that gripe about the neck and confinement of the head, the proneness to which was the most devilish characteristic of this ugly engine." She has an infant in her arms, and what with this and "the heavy weight of a thousand unrelenting eyes," is really burdened down. There she poses with her chin up for hours, while it gradually dawns on the reader that she has sinned and is being punished.

Some time earlier, it seems, Hester was married in England to a gentleman old enough to be her father, or even grandfather, a man with "a pale, thin, scholar-like visage, and eyes dim and bleared by the lamplight." His left shoulder was higher than his right, which was no help either to his looks or to his tailor. What attracted Hester to him Hawthorne does not explain, probably because he was unable to figure it out himself.

Two years before, Hester's husband had sent her to America, saying he would be along later. But he never arrived. Naturally, she assumed he was dead. How was she to know that he had indeed come to America but had fallen into the hands of Indians, who detained him nearly two years, trying to decide whether, with his thinning hair, he was worth scalping?

After a year or so, Hester had grown tired of waiting and had given birth to a child. There was strong suspicion that she had had an accomplice. But who? Everyone was busy guessing. The suspense was mounting, and so was the anxiety of young men about town, improper Bostonians unable to think up an alibi.

Now, standing on the platform, Hester stares back proudly at the curious Puritans. Suddenly she sees an elderly

Worth scalping?

man whom she recognizes by his "furrowed visage" [1] and by the fact that his left shoulder is a trifle higher than his right. It is her husband! He bends his eyes on her and she fastens hers on him. She clutches her sin-born infant to her heaving bosom until the poor thing is in danger of becoming seasick. Meanwhile her husband's face darkens and "a writhing horror," having "twisted itself across his features," slithers off into the bushes. It gives you the creeps.

Before being returned to prison, Hester is exhorted by the Governor (a political hack who ran on the Puritans First ticket) and other somber dignitaries to confess who is the father of her little bastard. One of the righteous gentlemen who lecture the erring woman is her pastor, the Reverend Arthur Dimmesdale, a nice young clergyman who has large

[1] He was run over by a plow.

brown melancholy eyes and "a mouth which, unless when he forcibly compressed it, was apt to be tremulous." His mouth is wobbling like jelly when he asks Hester to name her baby's father. Thereupon, lo and behold, her sin-baby lifts up its little arms to the minister so appealingly that one begins to wonder. No, it *couldn't* be!

"Da-da!"

Back in prison, Hester is visited by her husband, Roger Chillingworth, a cold fish whose name fits him better than his clothes.

Hester is in a state of nervous excitement, and the child, "who, drawing its sustenance from the maternal bosom, seemed to have drunk in with it all the turmoil, the anguish and despair, which pervaded the mother's system," is sick to its little stomach. Chillingworth opens his leathern case and gives Hester and her baby a draught he learned about from the Indians. Hester quaffs it without even glancing at the label, she is that trusting. No wonder the girl is in trouble.

Chillingworth is no M.D., and has had only a basic course

in alchemy. Moreover, his bedside manner leaves much to be desired. Instead of asking Hester how she feels, he asks her who is the father of her child.

"Ask me not!" replies Hester, who is never without an exclamation point. "That thou shalt never know!"

Chillingworth swears he will find her lover. "He bears no letter of infamy wrought into his garment, as thou dost," he hisses, "but I shall read it on his heart." He probably learned how to do this from the Indians, too. Meanwhile Hester must promise not to disclose to anyone that Chillingworth is her husband.

"Breathe not the secret, above all, to the man thou wottest of," says Chillingworth menacingly and then, picking up his leathern case, oozes out. He is up to something, though Hester wots not what.

When her prison term is over, Hester goes to live in a little thatched cottage on the outskirts of town. You'd think she would clear out of there and go to New York or somewhere more congenial to sin. But no, she stubbornly sticks around, for the good of her soul and Hawthorne's plot. She makes her living plying her needle, with which she is so felicitously diligent that she makes no distinction between work and ply.

Always she wears a scarlet letter on her blouse. Research has failed to reveal exactly how she managed it. Did she have one special blouse for show, so to speak, with a scarlet letter on it? Did she have half a dozen blouses, each with its letter? Or did she have one letter, which was detachable and could be switched from blouse to blouse? This is the sort of problem that makes literary scholarship so fascinating.

With Hester lives her child, named Pearl.[1] As time passes,

[1] Perhaps because she is slightly unstrung.

Half a dozen blouses?

she grows into a difficult little girl who is forever asking her mother embarrassing questions about the scarlet letter. As Freud could have told Hester in a minute,[1] her daughter is clearly manifesting a latent consciousness of sex. Townspeople think Hester a bad influence, and the Governor, who seems to have no more important state business, is about to take Pearl from her mother when the Reverend Mr. Dimmesdale intervenes, his mouth wobbling like mad. Henceforth he clutches his heart each time he speaks, and one need not be a cardiologist to know that the old ticker cannot stand this sort of mauling for long.

Meanwhile Roger Chillingworth, the wronged husband, remains in town, setting himself up as a physician without a license. His professional services are welcomed, because the only other surgeon is the local barber, who can start a flow of blood but has difficulty stopping it. Chillingworth's favorite patient is the sickening Mr. Dimmesdale,[2] who is

[1] Though, to justify his fee, he would have taken considerably longer.

[2] There are some who think Dimmesdale absolutely nauseating.

getting paler and thinner every day, in part because of his practice of fasting "to keep the grossness of his earthly state from clogging and obscuring his spiritual lamp." [1] Since he continues to decline, "Doc" Chillingworth applies leeches to his veins, where they slurp away merrily. Poor Mr. Dimmesdale fails to become more robust, but the leeches grow so fat they can hardly waddle off to the next patient.

Chillingworth now moves in with the young preacher, not merely to save house calls but to make it possible for him "to go deep into his patient's bosom, delving among his principles, prying into his recollections, and probing everything with a cautious touch, like a treasure-seeker in a dark cavern." Sigmund Chillingworth may have no medical degree, but all that time he claims to have spent with the Indians he was probably in Vienna.

In short, Chillingworth is beginning to think Mr. Dimmesdale is his man. One day, coming on the preacher while he is napping, he unbuttons the fellow's vestments

[1] What he needs is a new wick.

His favorite patient

and takes a look at his chest. Hawthorne does not tell us what he saw that caused such a wild expression of wonder, horror, and joy. Mayhap his patient's id, for which he had been groping these many weeks, had surfaced for air. At any rate, he is convinced that (1) the Reverend Mr. Dimmesdale is Pearl's father and (2) perseverance pays.

Now, without letting him know he knows, Chillingworth gives his patient the full treatment. This includes feeding him vitamin-rich weeds he picks from the tops of graves. Mr. Dimmesdale, responding encouragingly, gets worse and worse. He takes to looking at himself in the mirror under a green light. He also lashes himself across the shoulders with a bloody scourge he keeps in his bloody scourge closet. When the weather is thoroughly foul, he goes for a walk all unbuttoned.

One particularly ugly night Mr. Dimmesdale goes walking in strange company. He is pushed along by Remorse and pulled back by her sister, Cowardice, probably a couple of tipsy parishioners. Suddenly he finds himself at the foot of the scaffold on which Hester earlier had displayed her red badge, discouraged. Mounting it, he vows to confess his sin at last, knowing full well that it is too dark for anybody to see him and that the townspeople have been in bed since 9 P.M.

Beastly night as it is, Hester and Pearl just happen by, and Mr. Dimmesdale invites them up onto the platform. There they join hands in a circle and make a pretty family picture, a fine example of Togetherness.

"Wilt thou stand here with Mother and me, tomorrow noontide?" inquires Pearl with her usual knack for asking embarrassing questions.

"Nay, not so, my little Pearl," replies the minister, who is inclined to procrastinate. He suggests a somewhat later date, such as Judgment Day.

About this time there is a meteor flash, and Mr. Dimmesdale thinks he sees a great scarlet A in the sky.[1] He may only be imagining things. However, he actually does see Roger Chillingworth, who all the while has been lurking in the bushes with pad and pencil. Chillingworth, a combination roving reporter and house detective, is always on hand when anything interesting happens. He was even in the closet when Mr. Dimmesdale was whipping himself, hiding behind a pile of surplus surplices.

But Mr. Dimmesdale's secret shame is still not revealed to the public. Chillingworth, who fancies himself a sort of colonial Marquis de Sade, wants to torture the sinner for a while. Thus seven years pass, with no more than the turn of a page. Hester is becoming tolerated locally. People have got so they even say "Howdy, thou" to her, but she

[1] It was a red-letter night.

Hester tolerated

puts her finger to her lips and points to her bosom. Far from being ashamed, she seems proud.[1]

While Hester has been getting almost unbearably saintly, Chillingworth has turned into a devil. "There came a glare of red light out of his eyes," Hawthorne says. Hester goes to him and begs him to stop persecuting Mr. Dimmesdale. Look what it is doing to his own bloodshot eyes. But Chillingworth laughs ("Ha! ha!") in her face. He is enjoying himself. However, Mr. Dimmesdale has run out of laughs, now even scourging himself listlessly.

All this time Hester, who is better than most women about keeping a secret, has not told Mr. Dimmesdale that Roger Chillingworth is her wronged husband. But one day, meeting the minister in the woods, she tells him, and he is taken aback aplenty. His physician! His roommate! Come to think of it, the fellow *has* been acting a little odd, chuckling in that pleased way every time his patient has a heart attack.

After seven lean years, Mr. Dimmesdale decides he has had it. A ship for England is in harbor, and he and Hester and Pearl will flee to the Old World and start life anew. He begins to pack his vestments, and Hester fills a suitcase with needles.

It looks as if they are to escape. While Hester is happily planning to toss the Scarlet Letter into the ocean, Mr. Dimmesdale, in a burst of enthusiasm and fellowship, has the impulse to tell one of his parishioners a dirty joke. Unfortunately the impulse passes before he can think of one.

Now, alas, Hester learns from the shipmaster that he has booked another passenger for the voyage, one Chillingworth, Roger! This, we must agree, is a tough break. Of

[1] Of which, the letter or her bosom, Hawthorne does not make clear.

course they might drop Roger over the side in mid-ocean, along with the Scarlet Letter, but such a sensible solution does not come to mind. They can think only of dinner at the captain's table, or their morning constitutional around the deck, or a game of quoits or shuffleboard—with Chillingworth's demonic cackle in their ears and his bright red eyes peering from behind a life raft.

Fortunately, there is one way to get out of this apparent impasse, and Hawthorne takes it. As Mr. Dimmesdale strolls through the market place, receiving the congratulations of the townspeople on one of his most hypocritical sermons, he sees Hester and Pearl standing by the very scaffold on which they had stood in shame a couple of hundred pages back. Seized by an impulse,[1] he mounts the platform, signaling them to join him. And who climbs up there with them, uninvited as usual? None other than Chillingworth, Roger!

The Reverend Mr. Dimmesdale now confesses. To wit, he sinned just one little sin, and look at all the trouble he caused. Thereupon he drops dead, but not before tearing open his shirt to bare his chest, on which some of the spectators later testify to having seen a SCARLET LETTER, exactly like Hester's! As to how it got there, opinions vary. A plausible theory is that it was caused by "the ever-active tooth of remorse, gnawing from the inmost heart outwardly," a little like a gopher. Then again it may only have been a rash.

After Mr. Dimmesdale's confession and demise, Chillingworth, having lost his only patient, gives up his medical practice. Gradually he shrivels up and, within the year, expires, or blows away. Hester disappears from the colony

[1] Hawthorne's—to end the novel.

Togetherness

for a while, but eventually comes back and spends the rest of her life Doing Good. She continues to wear the scarlet letter on her bosom, but now instead of a stigma it has become a tourist attraction.

When Hester dies, she is buried in the graveyard, where a single tombstone suffices for her and for Mr. Dimmesdale. With admirable succinctness, the only engraving on it is the letter A. We would fain commend such New England thrift.

Questions on *The Scarlet Letter*

1. If you saw a young woman today with an "A" on her bosom, would you think she was:

   a. Absolutely top grade?

   b. Going steady with an Amherst boy?

2. Conscientious though he was about his pastoral duties, did the Reverend Mr. Dimmesdale have to do *everything* himself? Didn't he have an assistant?

3. Hester is said to have made her living with her needle. Did she give inoculations on the side? If not on the side, in the arm?

4. Has it ever occurred to you that Pearl might have come out of an oyster?

5. What could Chillingworth have seen on Mr. Dimmesdale's chest that was so startling:

   a. An unusual amount of hair?

   b. Notes for a sermon?

6. Take two symbols and clash them together. Did you forget to keep your fingers in your ears?

7. What if Hester and her preacher friend had gotten away from Chillingworth and gone back to England? Could they ever have been truly happy, accompanied by Shame, Remorse, and Pearl?

8. For collateral reading, look up the stories of Hester, Rose, and Daisy in Van Wyck Brooks's *The Flowering of New England.*

HERMAN MELVILLE

Melville's ancestry was distinguished on both sides. His grandfather on his father's side was an "Indian" in the Boston Tea Party, though the real Indians recognized him at once by his quotation marks. His grandfather on his mother's side was the famous Gen. Peter Gansevoort. What he was famous for is not certain, perhaps for being descended from Harmen Harmense Van Gansevoort, a colonial brewer who forced a laugh every time someone said his bock was worse than his bite.

Herman was born on August 1, 1819, in New York City. It is interesting to note that Walt Whitman was born in the same year in West Hills, Long Island, and someone can probably make something of this, although it is hard to imagine what.

When Herman was twelve, his father went into bankruptcy, and when he did not come out after several months, people knew something was wrong. As a matter of fact, he had died. He left his wife and eight children virtually destitute, and Herman's mother, who thought this sort of thing should never happen to a Gansevoort, became hard to live with. "She hated me," was the way Melville put it, trying to explain why he never warmed up to Mother's Day.

Melville had no formal education after the age of fifteen, again showing how important it is not to be educated if you wish to become a famous writer. At seventeen he shipped as a cabin boy, bound[1] for Liverpool. After some months he returned to New York "with a taste for the sea that was never to leave him." It was a salty taste, with a slight tang of kelp, and explains the slightly unpleasant look which could be seen around Melville's lips until they disappeared behind a luxuriant beard.

After a short career as a schoolteacher, Melville again went to sea, probably because some busybody told the principal about his never having got beyond the eighth grade. This time he set out for the South Seas on the whaler *Acushnet* (named after a sneeze). When the ship put in at the Marquesas, a bevy of naked maidens swarmed aboard, and overcome by embarrassment, he jumped ship.

Eventually, after fighting his way through the lush tropical growth and enduring frightful nightmares in which naked maidens kept swarming aboard, Melville found himself in a village inhabited by the Typees, a savage tribe of cannibals. Though they did not consider him a captive, they de-

[1] And determined.

Melville and cannibal women

tained him. This meant that he could take off any time he wanted, if he did not mind being shot in the back with a poisoned arrow.

Melville was treated kindly by the cannibals and would have been pleased with the way he was plied with coconuts and papayas had he not noticed that Thanksgiving was ap-

Melville and chef

proaching. Casually inquiring of the chief whether he might perchance be intended as the main course, he was relieved when the head man replied, "No, you not the Typee," and then roared over his own joke until he almost split a loincloth.

While living with the natives, Melville was forced by a housing shortage to occupy the same hut with a lovely, dark-skinned beauty named Fayaway. He never married her, because he could not imagine her being called Fayaway Melville, or living in New York City, where the Gansevoorts would insist that she wear a blouse.

Unconvinced by the chief's assurances,[1] Melville got himself smuggled aboard an Australian whaler, disguised as a sack of breadfruit. Someone had thoughtfully written on the shipping tag, "This Side Up." Subsequently leaving the whaler, he wandered from one South Sea island to another. He was accompanied on his wanderings by a ship's physician, Dr. Long Ghost, who found it almost impossible to attract any patients.

Melville finally got back to the United States by joining the Navy, which saved him the price of the passage though it meant serving a two-year hitch. He was discharged in Boston, out of a small cannon used for separating from the service those who wished to get home quickly. His experiences on a man-of-war gave him the material for *White-Jacket,* a novel most people think is about a hospital attendant.

Melville's years at sea were, he once said, "my Yale and Harvard," except that he received no degree and no letters from the Alumni Fund. Around New York he came to be

[1] In Polynesian, the words "chief" and "chef" are interchangeable.

known as "the man who had lived with the cannibals," but the reputation earned him few dinner invitations.

His first books, such as *Typee* and *Omoo,* were extremely popular, but as his writing became more and more profound it was less and less understood. This depressed Melville, as also did his marriage to the daughter of the Chief Justice of Massachusetts. On muggy summer days she refused to sit for hours by his bedside, stirring up a breeze with a palm leaf, as Fayaway had done. He became gloomy and, some thought, insane. The latter view is substantiated by an impossible request he made while writing *Moby Dick:* "Give me a condor's quill! Give me Vesuvius' crater for an inkstand!" Later he went so far as to say that *Moby Dick* was "broiled in hell-fire," a statement that no one took seriously.

During his period of gloom, Melville met Hawthorne and was depressed still further. The two took long walks in the hills, discussing death, sin, and the Devil until they were too morbid for words, whereupon they sat on a couple of stones and stared at each other. Remembering these happy days, Melville dedicated *Moby Dick* to Hawthorne "in

Two morbid

token of my admiration of his genius," and was relieved to receive a letter from his friend stating that he did not consider this offensive.

By coincidence, Melville like Hawthorne was employed in a customs office. But Melville was "outdoor customs inspector" in New York, and probably saw more interesting customs outdoors in New York than Hawthorne saw indoors in Boston. Evenings, after hours, Melville did a curious thing, according to Lewis Mumford: "He drew back the cosy hangings of Victorian parlours, and disclosed the black night outside." Friends stared out at the pitch black for hours, as if fascinated, to humor him.

Melville died in New York on September 28, 1891, blissfully unaware that, in the years to come, so many people [1] would leave the hyphen out of *Moby-Dick*.

[1] Including the present writer.

Moby Dick

Before beginning his story, Melville gives the reader some fascinating information about whales, such as the fact that the word for whale in Danish is *hvalt*. This he learned, he says, from "a late consumptive usher to a grammar school." [1] Then he lists several pages of famous literary references to whales, one of which is: "This whale's liver was two cart-loads." By this time the reader can hardly wait to learn what is going to happen next.

"Call me Ishmael," Melville says. (He had never liked the name Herman.) "Whenever it is a damp, drizzly November in my soul," he continues, "I get to sea as soon as I can." So now he is off for an ocean voyage, his soul dripping as if it has sprung a leak.

"I stuffed a shirt or two into my old carpet-bag, tucked it under my arm, and started for Cape Horn and the Pacific." Few travelers, undertaking a journey of this length, have packed so quickly and so sensibly. Soon, "quitting the good city of old Manhatto" (which is a couple of hundred miles south of the good city of old Bosto), he heads for Nantucket, where he will take ship.

But before he gets to Nantucket, a port he has chosen

[1] Spending too much time with Danish dictionaries was what made him late. And maybe ill, too.

for sentimental reasons (it is where the first dead American whale was stranded), he spends a couple of nights in New Bedford. There he seeks lodging at the Spouter Inn, the décor of its lobby featuring an oil painting of a whale and a whaling ship tossed about in a hurricane. Patrons who do not get sick looking at the painting can try the bar in the next room.

The inn being full, Ishmael has to share a bed with a chap who turns out to be a bit unusual. He is a harpooneer from the South Seas who sells embalmed heads to pick up a little extra cash. Ishmael is terrified by the fellow's purplish head [1] and strange tattooing, some of it in anatomical areas not usually devoted to works of art. But even though the savage, whose name is Queequeg, smokes a double-purpose tomahawk-pipe before dropping off to sleep, they get along fine. After all, he might have taken his harpoon to bed with him.

[1] His own. Those for sale are dark brown.

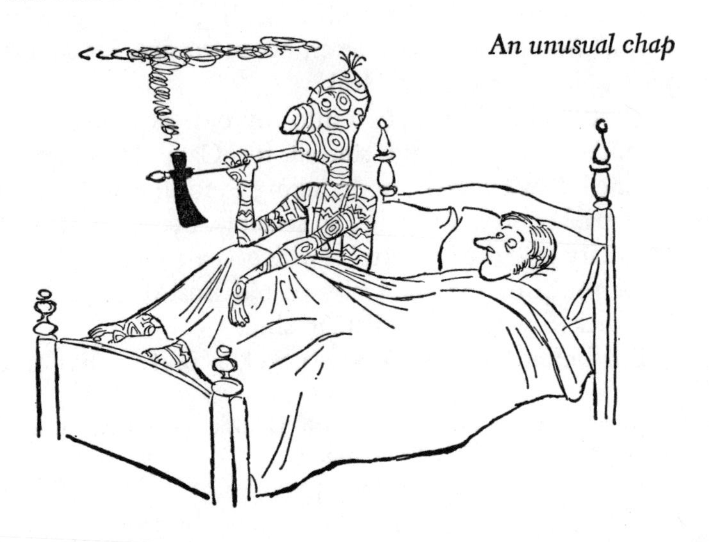

An unusual chap

The next day Ishmael, seeing the sights in New Bedford, comes to the Whaleman's Chapel. This is a cheerful place of worship, its walls decorated by marble tablets in memory of sailors lost overboard or killed by whales. The preacher, Father Mapple, climbs into the pulpit by a rope ladder, which he then pulls up so that no one can get at him if his sermon is too long. He addresses his congregation as "shipmates," and at the conclusion they should have said "Aye, aye" instead of "Amen," but Melville overlooked this ultimate nautical touch.

Ishmael and Queequeg become buddies. "It may seem ridiculous," Ishmael says fondly about Queequeg's head, "but it reminded me of George Washington's head, as seen in the popular busts of him." Ishmael is certainly right—about its seeming ridiculous.[1]

[1] On the face of it.

Ridiculous!

Ishmael and Queequeg now continue on to Nantucket, and their arrival at this island of fishermen provides Melville with an excellent opportunity to devote a chapter to the history of the fishing industry and another to clam chowder. This being before Nantucket became a tourist center, our author is deprived of such splendid subjects to digress upon as antique shops, shore dinners, middle-aged women in slacks, and the natives' snobbishness toward off-islanders. Reluctantly, he is forced to resume his story.

Ishmael and his companion sign on the whaling ship *Pequod,* chief owners of which are two retired sea captains, Captain Bildad and Captain Peleg. Both of these gentlemen are Quakers, as can be guessed from the way they "thee" and "thou" all over the place, and are opposed to killing anything. (Except whales.) Captain Peleg has trouble getting Queequeg's name straight, calling him Hedgehog and Quohog, and this affords comic relief. It is an even greater relief when Melville passes up a tempting chance to show what Queequeg could do with names like Bildad and Peleg.

In an interesting side remark about the name of the ship, Melville says: "Pequod, you will no doubt remember, was the name of a celebrated tribe of Massachusetts Indians, now extinct as the ancient Medes." [1]

As they are about to board the *Pequod,* Ishmael and Queequeg are stopped by an odd character named Elijah,[2] who hints darkly (did you ever know anyone to hint lightly?) about the *Pequod* and its skipper, Captain Ahab. He reminds one a little of the soothsayer in *Julius Caesar,* but this resemblance is lost on Queequeg, who apparently

[1] Frankly, I had not remembered until this very moment. Now I am trying to place the Medes.

[2] Some novelists use the telephone book to find names, but Melville just thumbed through the Old Testament.

isn't up on Shakespeare or the ides of March. The reader, however, knows that there is trouble ahead.

We seem about to be introduced to this Captain Ahab in Chapter XXII, but Melville, not wishing to rush things, elects at this point to give an account of the history and literature of whaling. Of course you knew all along that Louis XIV outfitted several whaling ships at his own expense,[1] that Alfred the Great wrote the first narrative of a whaling voyage, and that the grandmother of Benjamin Franklin was Mary Folger, who had something or other to do with the whaling industry. Nevertheless, you are grateful to be reminded of these facts, and the story can wait.

Melville now introduces us, one by one, to Starbuck, the chief mate; Stubb, the second mate; Flask, the third mate; and Tashtego and Daggoo, the harpooneers. Finally, being unable to put it off any longer, he tells us that one day while Ishmael was "levelling his glance at the taffrail" (not an

[1] Vintage wines served with the officers' *pâté de foie gras,* no doubt.

Interested in whaling

easy thing to do, on a rolling ship), there stood Captain Ahab on the quarter-deck.[1]

Ahab is a man you could easily identify in a police line-up. He has a white scar that runs from his hairline to his collar, and the rumor is that it goes all the way to the soles of his feet, though no one knows for sure, since he always takes a shower by himself. The other unusual thing about him is that he has a wooden leg made of ivory and steadies himself on deck by sticking this leg into a specially prepared leg-hole.

Easily identified

AHAB

Ahab is grim, troubled, mysterious. We are about to learn what is eating him (see the missing leg, above), when Melville suddenly thinks we should have a little lesson in cetology, about the Right Whale, the Wrong Whale, and all the other varieties. "I promise nothing complete," says Melville. "My object here is simply to project the draught of a systematization of cetology." That is why he has relatively little to say about such species as the Hump Back, the Razor Back, the Sulphur Bottom, the Thrasher, and the Grampus (an elderly type), and merely mentions the Bottle Nose Whale, the Pudding-Headed Whale, the Junk Whale, and others whose names indicate the descriptive powers of cetologists. After all, he must hurry on to a discussion of

[1] A small area, one-fourth full size.

mastheads, from Egyptian times to the present, ere he can resume his narrative.

At last the secret is out. Ahab's leg was crunched off by a great white whale with a wrinkled brow and a crooked jaw and three holes in his starboard fluke. The whale's name is Moby Dick, and he is easy to recognize, once you figure out which side is the starboard and swim up close enough to count the holes. Ahab has an obsession about avenging this loss of a member.[1] In a moment of frenzy and extravagance he nails a gold doubloon to the mast, the coin to go to the first to sight Moby or, we may assume, the first up on deck after dark with a claw-headed hammer.

Reader, hast ever known the monotony of day after day, week after week, month after month, with nothing to see but sea? Hast ever been on shipboard with a mad captain, stomping around all night on the deck over your bunk with an ivory leg? Can ye imagine a voyage with no social chairman, no shuffleboard, no betting on the ship's pool, no Captain's Dinner? Indeed, can ye imagine Captain Ahab with a paper cap on his head, whirling a noisemaker and tossing confetti?

Unless you are interested in a catalogue of famous pictures of whales, the manufacture of rope lines, the anatomy of the whale's eye, ear, and tail, how to skin a whale and cook the blubber, and the history of whaling from Perseus to the present, you would do well to turn from Chapter XXXVI to Chapter CXXXIII without further delay, thus saving nearly a hundred chapters without anybody's knowing the difference if you keep quiet. After all, Ahab isn't the only one entitled to be a skipper.

For now, after looking down from the mastheads, over

[1] A member in good standing, too.

the rails, and out of portholes, someone sees something. Unless by some coincidence there are two great white whales with wrinkled brows and crooked jaws and three holes in their starboard flukes, Moby Dick has finally swum into his own book. This, one feels, was bound to happen, but with only three chapters remaining, the reader can be forgiven for having been a little nervous. It is Captain Ahab who first spots Moby.[1]

"What d'ye see?" he cries to the other members of the crew, in Melville's words "flattening his face against the sky."

The others see nothing at first, except the oddly squashed face of their skipper, and Ahab goes out of his mind with excitement, shouting, "T'gallant sails!—stunsails! alow and aloft, and on both sides," and such gibberish. In his ecstasy

[1] Thus qualifying for his own gold piece on the mast, which makes the whole thing look rigged. But after all, as Melville says, the *Pequod* is a "rigged ship."

Moby Dick—at last

he even forgets and slips out of the gruff old sea captain's dialect, crying, "There she blows!" As even a landlubber is aware, the correct expression is "*Thar* she blows!"

But if you think Ahab is excited, listen to Melville. "Not the white bull Jupiter swimming away with ravished Europa clinging to his graceful horns; his lovely, leering eyes sideways intent upon the maid; with smooth bewitching fleetness, rippling straight for the nuptial bower in Crete; not Jove, not that great majesty Supreme! did surpass the glorified White Whale as he so divinely swam."

Avast there, shipmates, I've sighted a theory. Thar she blows, to starboard! Canst see her? By the great horn spoon, here she is: If Jupiter could disguise himself as a bull to carry off the voluptuous Europa, could he not just as easily slip into a whale costume to plague old Ahab? In other words, Melville is hinting broadly, in the above passage, that Moby Dick is not, as so many scholars maintain, the Myth of Indestructibility, the Christian Deity, Untrammeled Nature, the Puritan Conscience, William Shakespeare, or Charlie's Aunt—but Jupiter! [1]

To return to the story, the crew of the *Pequod* lowers the whaleboats and take after Moby Dick, Captain Ahab in the lead. But before they can toss their harpoons, the whale comes up under the skipper's boat and splits it to pieces. Moby is in a bad mood: "The sight of the splintered boat seemed to madden him . . . as the blood of grapes and mulberries cast before Antiochus's elephants in the book of Maccabees." The comparison is apt, though there may be an occasional reader who cannot, at the moment, recall the incident of Antiochus's elephants.

[1] Now that this is cleared up, once and for all, what will the Melville specialists do for a living?

Ahab—before his swim

Ahab is hauled aboard ship, and the hunt for Moby Dick goes on all that day and the next. On the second day Ahab's boat is upset again by the whale and the skipper breaks his leg. Fortunately it is the ivory one, and the ship's carpenter whittles him a new limb before you can say tibia-fibula. With all this dunking, however, the crew is getting short on dry clothing.

Dost wonder that the crew fished their monomaniac captain from the sea? Would ye have done the same, when ye could have sailed off and left him floundering in the foam? Think, oh reader, of how ye might have promoted Starbuck to skipper and drunk grog till groggy. And how, when ye had come home to port, ye would have attended memorial services for poor old Captain Ahab, and collected your share of his share of the rich cargo of whale oil. Think on't, and marvel at the loyalty and stupidity of the crew of the *Pequod*.

But as Melville puts it, in a precious piece of alliterative prose, "this pertinacious pursuit of one particular whale" continues. Ahab explains why: "I am the Fates' lieutenant." This clears things up considerably.[1]

Now Ahab paces restlessly about the deck, wearing a "slouched hat." No doubt by donning this old fedora, pulled casually over one eye, he hopes not to be recognized by Moby Dick, who would expect to find him in more nautical attire.

On the third day the whale is sighted again, the boats are lowered, and Ahab goes forth to meet his foe. "Forehead to forehead I meet thee, this third time, Moby Dick!" he cries, not realizing how ridiculously overmatched is his puny brow.

However, it looks as if Moby is beginning to tire. Certainly he must be weary of having harpoons stuck into him and boats bang on top of his head. So he rams the *Pequod* itself, and sinks her with all hands aboard. This is

[1] Except for those who had thought Ahab a captain.

The chase goes on

something he could have done three days before had it occurred to him.

Only Ahab's whaleboat is left afloat, surrounded by hopeful sharks. As an appetizer, they nibble on the oars until the edges are scalloped. But now the whale draws nigh again.

"From hell's heart I stab at thee; for hate's sake I spit my last breath at thee!" shouts Ahab, enraged at having been cheated out of going down with his ship. Thereupon he throws his harpoon at old Moby, hard enough, he thinks, to go through and come out the other side. He puts everything he has into it, following through beautifully.

Unfortunately, Ahab is so preoccupied with his form, and keeping his eye on his harpoon, that the line gets tangled around his neck. Apparently he forgot the simple precautions taught in Elementary Harpooning. But accidents will happen.

Suffice it to say that, catapulted out of the boat with the line tightening around his throat, he not only fails to finish the threatening speech he is making but is never heard from again.

Everyone is drowned but Ishmael, who floats around on an unused coffin which is not only buoyant but so gruesome that sharks are afraid to come close. Had Ishmael drowned also, instead of being left to tell the tale, Melville would have had a problem.

It should be added that the whole story is full of allegory and symbolism. Ahab stands for something, the sea stands for something, and Moby Dick, as we have already pointed out, stands for something. The reader has to stand for quite a bit, too.

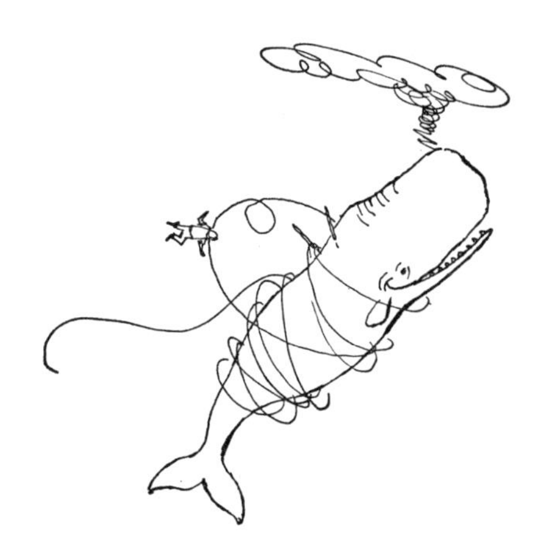

Questions on *Moby Dick*

1. What made Queequeg's head so purplish? Was he in the habit of holding his breath for long periods?

2. Was the Spouter Inn so called because of the tendency of fishermen to be extremely talkative after a few drinks?

3. How does a whaler demonstrate how big the one was that got away?

4. Is a starboard fluke a stroke of luck on the right side?

5. Have you ever had a strange craving for blubber? (If so, you might check your ancestry for Eskimo blood.)

6. How do you think Captain Ahab felt when he got his neck tangled up in his harpoon line?

   a. Pained?

   b. Embarrassed?

   c. Speechless?

7. Do you realize how much information you have picked up about whales? Has this made you any happier and better adjusted?

GEORGE ELIOT

George Eliot had a great deal of trouble with her name, and so have librarians ever since. Frequently her books are found under Mary Ann Cross, and not merely when a girl named Mary Ann Cross is sitting on them. Most readers, however, give up after searching for a few hours and read something by, say, Eliot, T.S.[1]

When she was born, on November 22, 1819, George Eliot was named Mary Ann Evans. The confusion began when everyone started calling her Marian. Then, when she lived with George Henry Lewes (more about this later, and we

[1] After a few hours with Eliot, T.S., some readers give up reading entirely.

can hardly wait), people like the milkman, the greengrocer, and the chimney sweep, trying to be polite, called her Mrs. Lewes. She became Cross after Lewes died.[1]

How she became George Eliot is not clear. It may be that she got the idea from George Sand, otherwise known as Amantine Lucile Aurore Dupin, Baronne Dudevant. Or she may have taken the George from George Henry Lewes, who would not let her have his last name and had a first name to spare. Then again, she may have liked the By George on the title page of her books.

George was mixed up from the first. "She had the mind of a man and the heart of a woman," says one scholar, who might have gained a wide readership had he continued this anatomical analysis to the end.

In her formative years she lived with her family in a house called Griff. Then she moved to one more suitable, named Bird Grove. She was a homely young woman with a square jaw, a long nose, and an enormous head which looked as though it belonged on someone else. Prim and proper, she loved to discuss the latest book by Carlyle or Emerson, whose moral tracts she thought more fun than a church picnic.

A change came in George's life when she met Charles Bray, a prosperous ribbon manufacturer and amateur phrenologist, whose eyes almost burst from their sockets when he got his first glimpse of her cranium. He had never seen anything like it, even on a horse, and let his ribbon business go to hell while he took George up to London with him to have a cast made. It was all perfectly proper, because Bray's wife went along to chaperon and to help hold George's head down in the plaster of Paris.

When not checking head spans, Bray was busy writing

[1] That is, she married a Mr. Cross.

freethinking books. "The best things in life are free," he liked to say. When anyone offered him a penny for his thoughts, he was insulted. Under his influence, George stopped going to the family church and became interested in sects.

This led her in 1851 to a liaison with a writer and intellectual named George Henry Lewes, who was married but looking around. He was a short, slight man with sloping shoulders, described by Douglas Jerrold as "the ugliest man in London." The moment he saw George he realized that they were made for each other.

So it was that George and George came to live as man and wife, although it is not clear which was which. George's freethinking friends were shocked at her living with a married man, because they only advocated such things and had no idea of practicing them. But Lewes was good to George, putting up with her positivism and encouraging her writing by hiding all the bad reviews. He had written two highly unsuccessful novels himself, and thus was able to be of

The two Georges

great help as a critic of her work. Though many thought them an odd pair, they had much in common, such as headaches and indigestion.

When she became a famous author and was able to support Lewes, he grew more and more devoted to her. He thought it frightfully sporting (as it was) when she also undertook to support his wife and children. "Let George do it," he said, shrugging his shoulders. At times his enthusiasm led him to consider divorcing his wife and marrying George. But, not wishing to be impetuous, he continued their rather informal arrangement year after year until he suddenly died of old age.

George, then sixty, married John Cross, the son of a friend of hers, who was twenty years her junior. He was only one year her husband, however, because she took a chill at a concert (caught in a cross draft between the woodwinds and brasses) and died on December 22, 1880.

Many thought her novels were written by a man. But Dickens, we are told, detected her sex. Some say he came right out with it and asked George Henry Lewes, who was in a position to know, despite what you think of the Victorian Era.

A surprising number of people didn't care.

Silas Marner

George Eliot wrote this moral tale to prove that everything comes out all right for nice people, at least in the novels of George Eliot. It may take a little time, say thirty or forty years, but virtue will be rewarded, sinfulness will be punished, and everyone who hasn't already died a tragic death will live happily ever after.

Silas Marner, a linen weaver, lives alone in a stone cottage among the "nutty hedgerows" [1] near the village of Raveloe

[1] They're really crazy.

Silas

and not far from a deserted stone pit. From long years at the loom, Silas has grown pale, nearsighted, and so pathetic that the reader whose heart bleeds easily should keep a tourniquet handy. Aloof and antisocial, he occasionally falls into a trance or down a well.

Fifteen years before, Silas had come from a place called Lantern Yard, where he had been a happy, churchgoing type, engaged to an attractive young servant-woman. But when his best friend stole some money from the deacon, planted evidence to make the blame fall on Silas, and then married Silas's girl, his milk of human kindness lost some of its butterfat content. Sore annoyed, he moved to Raveloe, where he was in no hurry to cultivate the human race.

Working at his loom sixteen hours a day, seven days a week, untroubled by unions or by church membership, Silas becomes interested only in accumulating money. He has two leather bags full of guineas which he keeps in a hole under the floor. Every night he takes out his gold coins and runs his fingers fondly through them. Piling them in heaps and heaping them in piles, he has more fun than a bank teller.

"His life," says George Eliot, "was narrowing and hardening itself more and more into a mere pulsation of desire and satisfaction." He is, in a word, becoming a Miser. If something doesn't happen to change his sense of values, he is going to develop into something even worse, such as a Millionaire.[1]

Leaving Silas, we turn, all unsuspecting, to the people of the nearby village. The leading citizen of Raveloe is Squire Cass, whose house is full of guns, whips, pipes, tankards,

[1] Yet he has a heart of gold, though it is just as well he does not know, or he would have it out, fondling it.

Squire Cass and sons

and foxes' brushes. (It takes a brave and agile man to brush a fox.) The Squire's eldest son, Godfrey, is "a fine, open-faced young man" whose one weakness (perhaps because of that opening in his face) is drink. But one weakness, as we shall learn, is too many. The Squire's second son, Dunstan, is a rotter who carouses, bets, and sneers in his beer. Dunstan has a hold over his elder brother, because the latter has lent him some of the Squire's rent money, which Dunstan has lost in gambling. Also Dunstan is the only one who knows Godfrey is secretly married to an ex-barmaid who takes laudanum.[1]

Were Dunstan to tell all, or even half, Godfrey would truly be in disfavor with the Squire, who has not envisioned quite this sort of daughter-in-law. Even worse, it would break up Godfrey's romance with the beautiful Miss Nancy

[1] This could be why Dunstan got the loan, without collateral.

Lammeter, "who has been looking very shyly at him ever since last Whitsuntide twelvemonth." In another Whitsuntide or two she may be able to look him straight in the eye, and then there is no telling what might ensue.

Godfrey's secret wife [1] is obviously in the way.[2] He rues the moment of drunkenness when he was urged into the marriage which has become a blight on his life. "Damn!" (the Curse of Drink) he says to himself. When Dunstan threatens to tattle unless he is given more money, Godfrey bites his lips and clenches his fists.

"Don't come near me with that look," he threatens, "else I'll knock you down." Another time, pallid with rage, he cries, "Hold your tongue, you fool, else I'll throttle you." There is always an alternative, else there might have been fisticuffs.

Godfrey is fast becoming embittered. He even rejects his brown spaniel, Snuff. In her warm, lucid style, George Eliot explains: "The yoke a man creates for himself by wrong-doing will breed hate in the kindliest nature."

No longer able to postpone paying back the rent money, Godfrey knows not where to turn. His secret marriage, he feels, is "the bit that Destiny had put into his mouth." It must be this metaphor that reminds him of his horse, Wildfire, which he tells Dunstan to offer up for sale. So Dunstan rides off on the mare. After taking a draught of brandy from (look it up for yourself, in Chapter IV) "his pocket-pistol," apparently a six-shooter containing six shots, Dunstan cannot resist the temptation to make Wildfire jump a few fences. The poor horse takes one fence too many,

[1] Godfrey's Secret Wife—what a wonderful name for a soap opera!

[2] In the family way, as a matter of fact.

Dunstan rides off

falls, and painfully pants his last. As luck would have it, Dunstan emerges without so much as a broken bottle.

As he walks disconsolately back to town, Dunstan passes near—were you wondering what had happened to him?—the cottage of Silas Marner. Having heard rumors of Silas's hoard of gold and finding no one at home,[1] he boldly enters to have a look-see. "There were only three hiding-places where he had ever heard of cottagers' hoards being found: the thatch, the bed, and a hole in the floor," says George Eliot, who wants him to find the money and get out of there fast, before Silas returns. With one chance in three, he has the bricks up in a few minutes and makes off with the weaver's life savings.

[1] Silas had stepped outdoors for a few minutes. He might well have put a little of his money into plumbing.

When Silas discovers his hoard is gone, he is distraught. Here is one time when it isn't the principle of the thing, it's the money. He runs screaming to the Rainbow, the local pub, which is full of townsmen who speak in such a thick dialect (one of them says he'd "never see'd no ghos'es") that it's a wonder they understand Silas's pure English when he blurts out, "I've been robbed!"

Soon Raveloe is abuzz with the robbery. Nothing newsworthy having happened for years, the gossips have been desperate for something to monger. Silas, however, is crushed. Without his guineas to count at night, all he can do is lean his elbows on his knees, clasp his head with his hands, and moan. "He moaned very low—not as one who seeks to be heard." By not straining himself, he manages to moan through most of a chapter.

Among those who feel sorry for Silas, in addition to the reader, is the good-hearted Mrs. Winthrop, the wheelwright's wife, who rises at four-thirty every morning to put in a full day of comforting people. Some she routs out of a sound sleep for comforting. She is described as fresh-complexioned, with "her lips always slightly screwed, as if she felt herself in a sick-room with the doctor or the clergyman present." Usually she is and they are.

Mrs. Winthrop calls on Silas, taking him some lard-cakes, "flat paste-like articles, much esteemed in Raveloe," where indigestion is rife. She tries to get Silas to stop weaving on Sunday and go to church, but has no luck, for "the fountains of human love and divine faith had not yet been unlocked, and his soul was still a shrunken rivulet." It has been a dry summer.

Dunstan, by the way, has never been seen since the day Wildfire was killed and he stole Silas's money. No one stops to think that his disappearance may have something to do with the robbery. (In Raveloe, no one even *starts* to think.) Godfrey expects him home any day, sneering and leering and threatening exposure as usual. The cad!

With Dunstan away, Godfrey can court Nancy Lammeter a little more openly, though he still cannot marry that dear creature because of already having a wife.[1] Nancy of course has no idea of his secret marriage, but her discovery that his lips have touched liquor causes her to question whether she could ever marry a man "whose conduct showed him careless of his character." The girl is in for a real jolt.

On a chill New Year's Eve they are having a party at the Squire's house. While Godfrey is taking "draughts of forgetfulness from the sweet presence of Nancy," his Secret Wife, Molly by name, is walking with slow, uncertain steps

[1] And a poor husband he is, for he contributes not a farthing to keep her in laudanum.

Godfrey courting Nancy

through the snow-covered Raveloe lanes, carrying her child in her arms. "This journey on New Year's Eve was a premeditated act of vengeance," explains George Eliot, "ever since Godfrey, in a fit of passion, had told her he would sooner die than acknowledge her.... She would mar his pleasure: she would go in her dingy rags, with her faded face, once as handsome as the best, with her little child that had its father's hair and eyes,[1] and disclose herself to the Squire as his eldest son's wife." Molly seems untouched by the holiday spirit.

However, the uninvited guest never makes it. To warm herself, she lifts a vial to her lips and drinks a black potion. Then she lies down in the nice cool snow and takes a nap. As the reader might guess, they are near Silas's cottage.

"Mammy!" cries the little one, bringing a touch of the Old South to the English Midlands. Then, rising on its spindly legs, the tiny tot toddles through the snow, toddles

[1] Which will save all that folderol of a blood test.

Untouched by the holiday spirit

into the cottage,[1] toddles right up to the hearth, where it gurgles and coos and warms its little hands.

This is the first two-year-old to toddle into Silas's remote cottage of a midwinter eve. At first he thinks the child's golden hair is his hoard of gold, which has toddled back to him. But alas, he lifts a few locks and listens in vain for them to clink as they drop. The child's wet boots

He lifts a few locks

suggest that she has walked through the snow (Silas can make some very shrewd deductions when he puts his mind to it), and by following the little footsteps he finds the body of the mother. She has had a hard life, and now has come to a hard end, frozen stiff.

When Silas, the child in his arms, bursts in upon the New Year's party with news that he has found the body of a woman, Godfrey hopes it is his wife. He stops dancing with Miss Nancy Lammeter long enough to race through the snow in his pumps to have a look. Eureka! He's a widower! A Happy New Year, indeed!

[1] By sheer good luck the door is open on this wintry night.

As for the child, Silas becomes devoted to her. She seems to have been sent to him by what Mrs. Winthrop repeatedly refers to, looking up toward Heaven, as "Them." Unaccustomed as he is to naming children, he names her Hepzibah and tends her tenderly. "The stone hut," says our author, "was made a soft nest for her, lined with downy patience." Silas should stop weaving and take up interior decorating.

* * * * * * * * * * * * * * * *

It is now, as you can tell by the asterisks, sixteen years [1] since Silas Marner found his new treasure on the hearth. We shall recognize our old friends of Raveloe, as they come out of church of a Sunday morning, "in spite of Time, who has laid his hand on them all." Time has touched Godfrey Cass around the middle. Nancy, his wife, may have lost some of her bloom, but her soul is lovelier than ever. For, we learn, "often the soul is ripened into fuller goodness while age has spread an ugly film, so that mere glances can never divine the preciousness of the fruit."

Silas is bent and white of hair, now being all of fifty-five. Hepzibah, who is familiarly and sensibly called Eppie, is a blond, dimpled lass of eighteen.

Godfrey and Nancy have been happily married all these years, save that their union has not been blessed by children. Godfrey is thus punished for his sins by being denied the pleasures of hearing the patter of little feet or waiting to get into the bathroom or being sassed back by a know-it-all adolescent. It is, we are assured, "a privation to which he could not reconcile himself."

[1] Count those asterisks.

But now a dramatic discovery is made. The old stone pit has been drained of the water that has always stood in it, and what do you suppose is down there in the bottom? Dunstan! [1] It seems he fell in that night, many years ago, after robbing Silas. The years have not dealt as lightly with him as with the others, for he is now only a skeleton of his former self. Gone is his sneer, along with his face, but he is recognized by the hunting whip in what used to be his hand. By his side are Silas's long-lost guineas. It is fortunate for Silas that he hoarded coins instead of currency.

At last Godfrey confesses everything to Nancy. It is a little late, to be sure, but he tells her with manly frankness that the woman found dead in the snow was his wife, and Eppie is his daughter. Then he bows his head and waits for the blow to fall. Does Nancy clobber him with a bronze bust of Queen Victoria? No, she only wishes he had told her long ago. They could have adopted Eppie and she would have been a mother to her.

Godfrey could kick himself, if he were double-jointed and not wearing those heavy boots. As George Eliot says, "He had not measured this wife with whom he had lived so long." Perchance he had lost his tape measure, or was it his nerve?

But there is still time to make amends by adopting Eppie, who is a mere child of eighteen and has only recently stopped calling Silas "Mammy." The repentant couple hasten to Silas's cottage, where Godfrey owns up to being the father of Eppie and offers to take her off Silas's hands, where she must surely interfere with his weaving. But Eppie, an old-fashioned girl, spurns their proffer of wealth, social position, and good grammar.

[1] Your first guess, probably, was stones.

"He's took care of me and loved me from the first, and I'll cleave to him as long as he lives, and nobody shall ever come between him and me." Thereupon she cleaves firmly to poor old Silas, almost knocking him to the straw.

Mr. and Mrs. Godfrey Cass go back to their big house, empty save for heirlooms and servants, doomed to a life of ease.

Eventually Eppie marries good-hearted Mrs. Winthrop's good-hearted son, Aaron. "You won't be giving me away, father," she says just before they enter the church, "you'll only be taking Aaron to be a son to you." (Now you know how old *that* cliché is.)

Everything ends happily with a wedding party at the Rainbow, after which all the men of Raveloe, and not merely Silas, are weaving.

As for the moral of the story, George Eliot has proved conclusively that drinking and stealing will get you nowhere, except maybe to the bottom of a stone pit, under twenty feet of water; that a little sin (see Godfrey and the

Eppie cleaves to Silas

barmaid) goes a long way (397 pages); and that if you take care of a homeless waif for sixteen years she may marry some oaf whom you will have to support the rest of your life.

What gives weight to George Eliot's moralizing is her having lived in sin all those years with a married man. And look what happened to her. She became a famous author.

Questions on *Silas Marner*

1. Imagine working sixteen hours a day at a loom. Just imagine.

2. At the end of the day, would Silas have been

   a. Warped?

   b. Woofed?

   c. Pooped?

3. What would you do if you had a younger brother like Dunstan? Would you do it with a gun, a bottle of arsenic, or a knife?

4. When Wildfire trips on the fence and falls, George Eliot refers to her "painful pants." Could they have been a little tight around the waist?

5. If you were looking for a cottager's hoard and it wasn't in the thatch, in the bed, or in a hole in the floor, would you

   a. Give up?

   b. Call Sherlock Holmes?

   c. Go straight?

6. While Molly was lying there in the snow, wouldn't the furze have kept her warm?

7. Think of a better title for Dunstan's autobiography than *Sixteen Years in a Stone Pit.*

8. Honestly, haven't you sometimes confused Silas Marner with the Ancient Marner?

CHARLES DICKENS

But for Charles Dickens, it is unlikely that we would now have Dickens Societies, the adjective "Dickensian," or picture postcards of the Old Curiosity Shop. There would also be a bare spot, about three feet long, on the bookshelves of most of the better homes.

Charles Dickens was born in Portsea, England, on February 7, 1812, but moved to London when he was a small boy, taking his mother and father with him. Soon his father, who was a clerk in the Navy pay office, had his income reduced "out of some idea of economy on the part of the government." [1] As his family grew larger, his pay check

[1] A crazy idea, indeed, which has not been tried since.

grew smaller, a process which could not go on indefinitely without undesirable results. Articles of furniture were gradually sold, until members of the family had to eat, sleep, and hang their hats [1] in shifts. Books were pawned one by one, and Charles, an avid reader, sometimes hung about the pawnshop finishing a last chapter.

Finally the elder Dickens was put into the Marshalsea (a very damp prison) for failing to pay his debts. Although many years later Charles was to become deeply indebted to Fielding, Smollett, Goldsmith, Cervantes, and Defoe, he somehow managed to avoid the fate of his father.

Eventually the whole family, except for Charles, moved into the prison, wanting to be together and hearing that the food was really quite good and served to you in your own cell. Charles boarded out, because he had a job in a blacking factory pasting labels on blacking pots ("Black," "Blacker," and "Blackest"), but came home weekends, tapping gently on the bars.

Despite the coziness of the Marshalsea, Dickens wanted a home of his own. Jilted by his first love, a harpist named Maria Beadnell, he married Kate Hogarth, who was no good at the harp but played on his sympathy. Kate had a sad, droopy look and hair hanging down the sides of her head that reminded him of something. It was too late when he thought of what it was—a spaniel.

Shortly after he married Kate, according to Hesketh Pearson, he "formed an attachment" to Kate's younger sister, Mary. Pearson is not very specific about how or where, and it is perhaps just as well.

Dickens's first writings were sketches depicting London life which he wrote under the name of Boz. His illustrator

[1] Only one hook.

was an effervescent artist named Phiz. They dropped these abbreviated names when Dickens was mistaken for Samuel Johnson's friend and his illustrator for a soft drink. Out of these sketches came *The Pickwick Papers*.

Like Byron, Dickens awoke to find himself famous.[1] Soon he had signed up with three publishers and was writing like mad, with a printer always standing at his elbow to grab each page the moment he had scribbled the last line. He was wearing out goose-quill pens so fast that a call went out to the farmers of England to step up the production of geese. A man of enormous energy, Dickens by now was not only writing novels but running a newspaper, acting in plays, attending salons, and supervising his household, where, we are told, "not a nail was hammered in without his assent." Nor was a nail pulled without explicit instructions from Father.

Dickens was a short man with long, wavy locks that came down over his ears and, in time, a mustache and beard that made him look like Buffalo Bill. As soon as he became wealthy from writing about the poor, he affected fancy

[1] A good reason for writers to go to bed.

Writing books about the poor

frock-coats, bright waistcoats, voluminous satin cravats, jeweled pins, and tightly fitting trousers strapped over pointed boots. He was, in a word, a dandy.[1] One of his contemporaries says that he had "an odd trick of sucking his thumbs while thinking." It is to be hoped that he did most of his thinking in private.

His works, such as *The Pickwick Papers*, came out a chapter a month and therefore could be purchased on the installment plan. Readers were always kept in suspense, wondering what would happen in the next chapter, but they were not half so worried as Dickens, who had no idea either. *Oliver Twist* was the first work in which Dickens "displayed his amazing power of capturing the atmosphere of London," each copy being hermetically sealed. In far corners of the earth, anyone with his nose in a book was probably an Englishman, nostalgic for the familiar stenches of the East End.

Though Dickens was becoming a great success in the literary world, all was not well at home. He was extremely neat, while his wife was a casual housekeeper who changed the antimacassars only once a fortnight. If the parlor was usually in bad shape, so was she, for she was almost always pregnant.[2] Despite being an Eminent Victorian, Dickens was only human. He became infatuated with an actress, Ellen Ternan, whom he established in a love nest and plied with gifts.[3] "Next to writing," says one biographer, "what he loved most was acting." Obviously this slipshod scholar meant to say "actresses," and should have read proof

[1] There are several other words, but this will do.

[2] She bore him ten children. Dickens kept telling her to stop, but she went right ahead.

[3] She was very pliable.

more carefully. At any rate, it was fortunate for Dickens that Queen Victoria never heard about all this.

Despite having a wife on his hands and a mistress in his arms, Dickens kept writing furiously. He became famous for his realistic descriptions and his attention to little things, such as Little Dorrit, Little Nell, and Tiny Tim. He also became known for his deathbed scenes, which occupy the last hundred pages of almost all his novels and were responsible for the enlargement of tear ducts throughout England and America.[1]

A humanitarian and a social reformer, Dickens was intensely concerned about the poor. It grieved him that they might not be able to buy his books. He felt that the rich should be forced to give up some of their ill-gotten gains, and for this reason was constantly trying to force his publishers to give him a larger share of the profits. He was not exactly mercenary, but when his publishers saw him coming they hurriedly changed into threadbare jackets, penciled dark circles under their eyes, and hid the day's receipts.

Dickens made two trips to America. The first gave him the materials for *Martin Chuzzlewit*, in which he described his hosts as humbugs, braggarts, savages, and idiots, thus setting a precedent for visiting Englishmen that is still honored today. His second trip, a lecture tour, made him rich. Having already convinced everyone that he could write, he gave public readings to prove that he could read. He was one of the first to give impersonations of Charles Dickens, and few have worked so hard at the part.

Our author had a wide circle of friends, which became

[1] They were also the cause of more than one lump in the throat, although, oddly, those so afflicted were the ones who swallowed Dickens's sentimentality most easily.

somewhat less wide each time he used one of them as the model for some villainous character. One friend, John Forster, remained loyal to the end in order to gather material for a four-volume biography.

Dickens died on June 9, 1870, at the age of fifty-eight, cutting Forster's work to three volumes. Though not a poet, he was buried in the Poets' Corner of Westminster Abbey. The Novelists' Corner could hold only a few famous novelists, all of them being rich and fat. But the Poets' Corner, into which poor and skinny versifiers could be crammed by the dozens, had room to spare.

Impersonations of Charles Dickens

David Copperfield

The story is told in the first person, by David Copperfield, though he is not born until the end of the first chapter. He has a remarkable memory, however, and remembers exactly how everyone looked and what everyone said during the argument between his mother, his aunt, and the doctor just before the delivery.

When David was born, he tells us, "The clock began to strike, and I began to cry, simultaneously." This probably does not mean that David was struck by the clock. However, it sets the tone of the book, in which somebody is always getting beaten and crying, although people frequently cry without being hit.

David's father died six months before David was born. This is the way he puts it: "My father's eyes had closed upon the light of this world six months when mine opened on it." Not only is this more delicate but it is recommended to any author who is being paid by the word. David's mother is a beautiful, baby-faced creature who married her late husband when she was half his age, which is probably why he called her his better half. Whenever anyone says a harsh word, her eyes fill with tears.[1]

David has a loyal friend in Peggotty, a plump nurse-

[1] They are small, and fill rapidly.

Peggotty

maid who is always hugging him and bursting the buttons off her dress. She is kept busy around the house, cooking, cleaning, and sewing on buttons.

Time passes. Once Peggotty takes David for a fortnight's visit to her brother's home, a fishing barge drawn up on dry land. It is almost as peculiar as the people in it. One of these is Peggotty's nephew Ham, whose name is wonderfully descriptive and whose laugh ("Hor! Hor!") is, fortunately, not contagious. Another is a Mrs. Gummidge, who speaks of herself as "a lone lorn creetur" and has a way of tugging at her own heart strings.

"Yon's our house, Mas'r Davy," says Peggotty as they approach, dropping two syllables for every one button. Among those David meets is Peggotty's niece, little orphan Em'ly, whose father has drownded and who feels sorry for all the poor fishermens and would like to help 'em if they was to come to any hurt. David falls in love with her immediately, doubtless fascinated by her bad grammar.

Returning home from the visit, David learns that his mother has married a Mr. Murdstone. As Peggotty tells him, with characteristic delicacy, "You have got a pa!" Thereupon, "Peggotty gave a gasp, as if she were swallowing something that was very hard." It is probably one of those Dickensian lumps in the throat.

Mr. Murdstone is tall, dark, handsome, and mean, and David takes an instant dislike to him. One senses the emergence of an Oedipus complex, but no reference is made to it, probably because Freud was born six years after the publication of *David Copperfield.*[1] Equally obnoxious is Murdstone's sister, Miss Murdstone, an uninvited guest who sits around stringing steel beads and urging her brother to be firm with David, which he has every intention of being.[2]

Mr. Murdstone, who wants his stepson to be well ed-

[1] Oedipus, however, had been around for centuries, and Dickens missed the scoop of a lifetime.

[2] Miss Murdstone, according to one critic, is "cut of the same cloth" as Madame Defarge, in *A Tale of Two Cities.* It is tough material.

The Murdstones

ucated, tries to beat David's lessons into him, using a cane instead of a book.

"Mr. Murdstone, sir!" cries David, polite even under stress, "don't, pray don't beat me!" Then, forgetting his manners, he bites the hand that beats him, and Mr. Murdstone is left with a scar that is going to be hard to explain.

So David is sent off to a boarding school near London, driven by a carrier [1] named Barkis. It is this gentleman who is responsible for the Famous Quotation, "Barkis is willin'," which is his romantic way of sayin' that he has no serious objections to marryin' Peggotty. He keeps waitin' and hopin'.

At the school, Salem House, David falls in with a student with the odd name (in anything but a book by Dickens) of Tommy Traddles and another named J. Steerforth. Steerforth is extremely popular, since he has influence with the headmaster, Mr. Creakle. He talks back to the teachers and even causes one of them, a rather decent chap, to be dismissed. A pupil of many accomplishments, Steerforth

[1] Whether of mail or typhoid, we are never told.

Steerforth has influence

is unquestionably a forerunner of Progressive Education.

Time passes.[1] One day David is summoned home because of the death of his mother, which makes him a full-fledged orphan, like Oliver Twist and many another Dickens youngster who goes on to better things. The funeral is suitably depressing, but the most gruesome episode is when, as David says, "Miss Murdstone, who was busy at her writing-desk . . . gave me her cold fingernails, and asked me, in an iron whisper, if I had been measured for mourning."[2] Miss Murdstone's detachable and refrigerated fingernails were a gift that should have delighted any red-blooded boy, but David does not so much as say thank-you.

Peggotty now takes David off to live with her kin, including little Em'ly, who is not so little as before and has soft "cherry lips," which go nicely with her apple cheeks. Peggotty and the persistent Barkis get married, because by now Peggotty also is willin'.

David is happy walking on the beach with little Em'ly, who looks up at him through her stray curls, blushing prettily. But Mr. Murdstone puts an end to this idling by sending the lad to London, to wash bottles for the firm of Murdstone and Grinby. It is not David's idea of a promising career,[3] and he is so unhappy that, as he says, "I mingled my tears with the water in which I was washing the bottles." Whether the solution was about fifty-fifty, or nearer sixty-forty, he fails to say.

While working at Murdstone and Grinby's, David lives with a Mr. and Mrs. Micawber. Mr. Micawber is so oppressed by financial troubles that one night he comes home to supper "with a flood of tears," wearing a life preserver,

[1] It has to, because the novel covers about thirty years.

[2] What a chance this gave David to reply, "No, ma'am, nor for evening either."

[3] All he can see is bottlenecks.

no doubt. At such a sight David himself is "dissolved in tears," and shortly afterward they are all so overcome that, says David, referring to Mr. and Mrs. Micawber, "he mingled his tears with hers and mine." It is easily the dampest scene in English literature until Somerset Maugham's *Rain.*

Mr. Micawber, though in and out of debtor's prison, is always sure that one of these days "something will be turning up." At heart an optimist, he smiles while he weeps, and goes around with a salty taste in his mouth.

Micawber

When the Micawbers move to another city and David has no one to cry with, he decides not to wash another bottle for Murdstone and Grinby but to run away to his Aunt Betsey Trotwood's in Dover. Thereupon ensues a harrowing journey in which the impoverished lad sells first his waistcoat and then his jacket and is lucky to get to Dover with his trousers.

At Miss Trotwood's, David comes to know Mr. Dick, who is even queerer than the usual Dickens character. Mr.

Aunt Betsey Trotwood

Dick lives upstairs and likes to fly kites. He also has an obsession about King Charles the First's head, or perhaps it is King Charles's first head. Whatever it is, it keeps getting into the Memorial he is writing and prevents his completing it, which is about as good an excuse as an unpublished author has ever been able to think up.

Miss Trotwood, who is too busy chasing donkeys off her lawn to have time for tutoring her nephew, sends him to Doctor Strong's school in Canterbury. There he boards with Mr. Wickfield,[1] a lawyer who drinks port all evening and has to be shown to his bedroom by his daughter Agnes who, being a teetotaler, always knows the way. Mr. Wickfield's assistant in the law office is Uriah Heep, who is continually grinding the palms of his cold, clammy hands against each other "as if to squeeze them dry and warm, besides often wiping them, in a stealthy way, on his pocket

[1] If you think the characters are beginning to pile up confusingly, just wait.

handkerchief." Anyone who anticipates shaking hands with Uriah would be well advised to carry a towel. Uriah is forever describing himself as "a very umble person," dropping his eyes and his h's indiscriminately.

One evening after David has had dinner with Uriah and his mother ("Thanks Heeps," he says as he leaves), whom does he see but Mr. Micawber walking by! A few days later he runs across his old schoolmate, J. Steerforth, at an inn!

A *very umble person*

England was very small in those days, or the laws of probability had not yet been passed.

Taking Steerforth with him, David, who is now an outstanding upstanding understanding young man of seventeen, goes to see his friend Peggotty. At first she fails to recognize him, but when she does, she cries out, "My darling boy!" and the next moment they are locked in a soggy embrace. It is just like old times.

The big news in the family is that Em'ly is affianced to Peggotty's nephew, the rough-hewn, thick-sliced Ham. A

shadow is momentarily cast over th
tha, a soiled woman who has been sha
to remind her of their days of inno
perhaps to get enough money to leav
truly pathetic, covering her face to hide
and making "a low, dreary, wretched moan
until Ham, who can stand it no longer, giv
savings. At this point Em'ly, too, sobs hyst
come either by Martha's plight or by her hus
depleted bank account.

But back to David. It is time for him to t
career, and his Aunt Betsey suggests that he becom
tor, a profession which he is immediately enthusiastic
though neither he nor the reader knows precisely wha
At any rate, he is to be articled to the firm of Spenlow
Jorkins, in London, and must pay a thousand pounds
the privilege. David's reaction to this drain on his aun
resources is so beautifully and unnaturally put that th
passage should be quoted in full.

"Now, my dear aunt," he says, "I am uneasy in my mind about that. It's a large sum of money. You have expended a great deal on my education, and have always been the soul of generosity. Surely there are some ways in which I might begin life with hardly any outlay, and yet begin with a good hope of getting on by resolution and exertion." [1] This causes his aunt to explain, in a couple of hundred well-chosen words, why she will be only too happy to spend the thousand pounds on her nephew.[2] Whereupon, over-

[1] One way would be to set up a school of elocution, where he might offer a course in How to Lay It On Thick.

[2] The reader can probably think of better ways for her to spend her money, such as building a fence around the lawn to keep off the donkeys.

by a wave of restraint, they neither embrace nor into tears.

vid's aunt sets him up in elegant quarters in London, e under the influence of Steerforth and liquor he be- es (dare we use the word?) drunk. Attending the the- in this deplorable condition, he has the bad luck to sit nt behind Agnes Wickfield, who has come to London, ne to the theater, and chosen this very seat, all for the ke of Dickens's plot.

"Lordblessmer! Agnes!" exclaims David thickly. He hinks he has ruined himself with Agnes, but that dear creature forgives him and invites him to dinner, no doubt to sober him up. She warns him against associating with that Bad Influence, Steerforth, and also tells him that Uriah Heep has her inebriated father in his power and is about to become a partner in the firm. In fact, as David learns later from Uriah's own unlovely lips, that slimy individual hopes to win Agnes also.

"Was it possible?" David asks himself, "that she was reserved to be the wife of such a wretch as this?" It is his first inkling that young women can be reserved, like seats at a theater, and he resolves to look into it.

David is invited for a weekend at the home of one of his employers, Mr. Spenlow, of Spenlow and Jorkins. Sure enough, Mr. Spenlow has a beautiful daughter, Dora, and sure enough, David falls in love with her. And who do you suppose is Dora's tutor? None other than Miss Murdstone, who has to get back into the story somehow. Forgetting about Em'ly and Agnes, David now can think of nothing but Dora. "I lived principally on Dora and coffee," he says, and becomes terribly lovesick, though it might be heart-burn. His housekeeper, Mrs. Crupp, a dialect character who

Dora and coffee

says "adwise" and calls David "Mr. Copperfull," tries in vain to cheer him up, or at least get him to eat something nourishing.

Now David's old schoolmate, Tommy Traddles, reappears, and so do Mr. and Mrs. Micawber, who are never more than a couple of chapters away. To David's distress, Mr. Micawber involves Traddles in a financial debt by using his name. Why anyone would want to use the name Traddles, even for monetary gain, is more than the reader can understand.

A great loss comes to David. Barkis dies. Or, as Dickens, writing fluidly, puts it, "It being low water, he went out with the tide." Another blow comes with the discovery that Em'ly has run off with Steerforth, who is now seen in his true colors (black and yellow). David is miserable, his

Runs off with Steerforth

heart being, as he says, "overcharged" with grief. There is nothing like being overcharged, unless it is being short-changed, to bring on a fit of despondency.

But David is not in low spirits for long. He goes on a picnic with Dora, and when she presses his bouquet "against her little dimpled chin," David is driven into a series of the shortest and simplest declarative sentences in all Dickens: "I don't know how I did it. I did it in a moment. I had Dora in my arms. I was full of eloquence. I never stopped for a word. I told her how I loved her. I told her I should die without her. I told her that I idolized and worshiped her." Rather than hear any more of this, Dora consents to becoming engaged, and the reader is everlastingly grateful to her.

But alas, just as things are going well for David, Miss Trotwood arrives at his chambers and announces that she has been ruined (financially). David, just to prove he is human, is downcast by the news that his aunt can no longer support him.

At this point, as if Dickens had somehow contrived it, Agnes rides up in a hackney-chariot. As David says, trying to get out the words before the lump in his throat renders him speechless: "A fair hand was stretched forth to me from the window, and the face I had never seen without a feeling of serenity was smiling on me." Good old Agnes! A friend in need! Though she reports that her father is now completely in the toils of Uriah Heep, who has become a full partner, she knows of a job for David. It seems that his old schoolmaster, Dr. Strong, last heard of seventeen chapters back, at this very moment is in need of a secretary who can work mornings and evenings—precisely the time David has available from his articling with Spenlow and Jorkins. What incredible luck!

"I was pretty busy now," David reports after taking this second job, "up at five in the morning, and home at nine or ten at night." But, to speed the day he can afford to wed dear, dear Dora, he decides to study shorthand between midnight and 5 A.M.[1] His friend Traddles optimistically tells him that "it might be attained, by dint of perseverance, in the course of a few years."

Things now going better, we can be sure they will shortly go worse. Miss Murdstone, who fancies herself a private eye, discovers David's impassioned letters to Dora and reveals to Mr. Spenlow that this upstart hireling dares to love his daughter. The ambitious cad! Mr. Spenlow thereupon gives David a tongue-lashing, leaving him with welts

[1] The reader who puts in only a forty-hour week should feel ashamed of himself.

Miss M. reads David's letters

across his psyche. Miss Murdstone, who would have loved bearbaiting, looks on in happy silence, though once she "laughs contemptuously in one short syllable." Dickens does not say whether it was "Ha," "Hee," or "Ho."

But the haughty Mr. Spenlow gets his. That very night, though there has been no previous hint of ill health, he drops dead. Still more shocking, his personal records reveal that he is not rich, after all! At one stroke (the one suffered by her father) Dora becomes (a) poor, and (b) an orphan like everyone else.

At this point let us quote the critic who said, "The plot of *David Copperfield,* to the student who compares it with most modern fiction, may seem almost incoherent." It will be seen, in what remains, that the word "almost" can be safely ignored.

For now, one snowy night in London when David is walking home, he almost bumps into—Em'ly's uncle!

"Well met, well met," the old fellow says repetitiously.

"Well met," answers David, who has a gift for mimicry.

Inasmuch as Em'ly's uncle has been wandering all over England, France, Italy, and Switzerland, looking for his niece and that blackguard Steerforth, it is truly extraordinary that he should find David instead.

But back to David and Dora. They are wed and live idyllically, she calling him Doady (having given up trying to pronounce David) and he calling her Child Wife and Little Blossom (having given up his brains). To anyone but the young newlyweds, it is all a little nauseating. David, having mastered shorthand, is now writing a book, dictating to himself at top speed. Dora, pretending to be his secretary, sits on his knee and holds his spare pens. With her precious curls and big blue eyes, she is as attractive a pen holder as you will ever see.

But what of Em'ly? She is found at last, and none too soon, because only a few chapters remain. She has left Steerforth, having learned after a few years that he was the rotter everyone else knew him to be in a few minutes.

A little nauseating

Her uncle finds her in London at Soiled Martha's, being browbeaten by Rosa Dartle, an old flame of Steerforth's who has loved him ever since the time he gallantly hit her in the mouth with a hammer. She has a disdainful way of speaking and a "curled lip." (See hammer blow, above.)

"What is there in common between *us?*" asks Rosa scornfully, wondering that Steerforth could have cared for both of them in the same delightfully brutal way.

"Nothing but our sex," says Emily. With this single candid observation, Dickens all but leaves the ranks of Victorian novelists. Anyhow, Em'ly is now back in the bosom of her family.

"Our future life lays over the ocean," says her uncle, telling Miss Trotwood of his plans for Em'ly and himself.

"They will emigrate together, aunt," David translates helpfully.

Disclosures and deaths now come thick and fast.[1] Mr. Micawber, who has been clerking for Uriah Heep, learns that Uriah has forged Mr. Wickfield's name and made off with Miss Trotwood's money. When confronted with his crimes, Uriah ceases being umble and, as David remarks, "throws off his mask." Without his mask, he looks worse than ever.

Back now, for the last time, to Dora. She is sickening and has to be carried up and down stairs. It is a strain on the reader and on David's back. Before long she dies ("a Blossom that had withered in its bloom"), and at the very same instant her dog Jip keels over. In view of all the other coincidences, this double demise is not to be deemed extraordinary.

[1] This is called the denouement, or "final disentangling of the intricacies of a plot." In Dickens it is usually the longest part of the book, there being so much to untangle.

In fact it is more than matched by a succeeding incident, when Ham loses his life in attempting to rescue a man from a shipwreck, and the man, whose corpse is washed up on the shore, turns out to be (no it *couldn't* be) (but it is) —Steerforth! David, by the way, happens to be on the beach at the moment, though it is his first time at the seashore in years. It is a bit of luck, for no one else could have identified the long-absent Steerforth, who is in no condition to speak for himself.

David goes abroad for three years, mailing back to England the articles and books his course in shorthand has enabled him to write. All of them are gratefully accepted by publishers, probably because they are eager to get the foreign stamps for their collection. Returning home, rich and famous, he discovers to his amazement that he loves Agnes. He is even more amazed to find that Agnes loves him, too. It is the most amazing chapter in the book.

"I folded her to my heart," David says, first reading the directions and carefully observing the dotted lines.

Happiness comes at last to David Copperfield. There would seem to be no more need for tears. But Dickens is not ready to throw in the towel, damp though it is. "Agnes," says David, "laid her head upon my breast and wept; and I wept with her, though we were so happy."

Although two chapters remain, let us leave them crying happily together and tiptoe away.

Questions on *David Copperfield*

1. *David Copperfield* is told in the first person. Singular, isn't it?

2. John Forster pointed out to Dickens that his initials, C.D., were the same as those of David Copperfield, only reversed. Try your best to understand the importance of this.

3. In always chasing donkeys off her lawn, wasn't Miss Trotwood making an ass of herself?

4. Whom do you hate the most:
   a. Mr. Murdstone?
   b. Miss Murdstone?
   c. Uriah Heep?
   d. Some member of your own family?

5. On which page did you shed your first tear? Did you know that some people are able to read Dickens only in the eighty-volume Absorbent Edition?

6. In the school David attended, which would a boy be most certain to get:
   a. A good education?
   b. A good flogging?

7. Mr. Micawber, the blowhard who served so much time in debtor's prison, is said to have been modeled on Dickens's father. Do you want your son to grow up to be a writer?

8. Compare the death of Dora with that of Little Nell in *The Old Curiosity Shop*, meanwhile whistling cheerfully.

9. Having finished *David Copperfield*, how do you feel? Full of the Dickens?

About the Author and the Illustrator

Richard Armour draws on a rich background for his satires of history and literature. A Harvard Ph.D., he has held research fellowships in England and France, has taught at such institutions as the University of Texas, Northwestern University, Wells College, the University of Hawaii, Scripps College (where he was also Dean of the Faculty), and the Claremont Graduate School, and has lectured or been guest-in-residence on more than two hundred campuses. He has lectured in both Europe and Asia as an American Specialist for the State Department.

After several scholarly volumes of biography and literary criticism, which he says he wrote "to get promoted," he turned to the satires and spoofs for which he is widely known. So far he has written thirty-seven books and contributed to some two hundred magazines in the United States and England, from *The New Yorker* and *The Saturday Evening Post* to *Look, McCall's,* and *Playboy*. His light verse is collected in such books as *Light Armour* and *Nights with Armour*. His prose satires include *It All Started with Columbus, It All Started with Eve, Twisted Tales from Shakespeare, American Lit Relit, Going Around in Academic Circles,* and *Through Darkest Adolescence*. And then there is that nostalgic-humorous account of his youth among the pills and potions, *Drug Store Days*.

Richard Armour is married, has two children, and lives in Claremont, California.

Campbell Grant, who has illustrated nine of Richard Armour's books, was with Walt Disney for twelve years as a character creator and story man. During World War II he worked with Frank Capra on documentaries. He is the illustrator of many books, for both children and adults, and has done the drawings for the book version of several Disney films. Living idyllically on a ranch near Santa Barbara, he raises avocados and has a talented writer-artist wife, four children, and one white burro.